How to Protect Your Child from Bullies

by

Dr Coral Milburn-Curtis

Copyright

ISBN 978-0-244-62564-1

ISBN 978-0-244-62564-1
90000

9 780244 625641

Acknowledgements & Notes

The inspiration for this work has come from several sources, but particularly from the many children and parents with whom I have worked over the years.

Their courage in overcoming the scourge of bullying has helped me to develop the anti-bullying techniques described in this book.

Every effort is made to maintain the accuracy of this material. If you find any errors or inaccuracies, please let the author know immediately at c.milburncurtis@oxfordalumni.org.

The book is written in the form of a practical workbook. It is written in British English, so please accept our apologies if any spellings 'jump off the page' at you.

This is a revised edition of the first edition of *How to Protect Your Child from Bullies*. This edition includes new and updated chapters, and references to the academic research that underpins the ideas on offer.

Dr Coral Milburn-Curtis, Author

Disclaimer

This book is not meant to be a substitute for medical, counselling or legal advice. The information provided is designed to provide stimulus for discussion on the subject of bullying.

If you are unsure about implementing any of the ideas presented in this workbook, then you should seek independent advice.

The book is not meant to be used, nor should it be used, to diagnose or treat any medical, psychological or emotional condition. For diagnosis or treatment of such, please consult your own professional.

The publisher and author are not responsible for any specific needs that may require legal or medical supervision and are not liable for any damages or negative consequences from any treatment, action, application or preparation, to any person reading or following the information in this book.

References are provided for informational purposes only and do not constitute endorsement of any websites or other sources.

Readers should be aware that the websites listed in this book may change.

About the Author

Dr Coral Milburn-Curtis DPhil (Oxon), MSc (Oxon), BA is a fellow of Green Templeton, University of Oxford. After teaching in England, South Africa and Magdalen College Oxford she took over the headship of the country's top primary school, leading it and two other primary schools for 10 years.

Once retiring from headship, Coral gained her doctorate from the University of Oxford, where her empirical research explored a range of educational topics including critical thinking and intellectual confidence in children.

During her time as a headteacher, she had gained a wealth of experience working with both children and parents, and developed a special interest in the notion of *protecting* children from the action and the outcomes of bullying.

Her academic research has confirmed her overwhelming conclusion that in order to protect our children from bullies, we should be focusing on building their confidence and resilience – since research has established time and time again that there is a strong and statistically significant relationship between an individual's self-esteem and their potential to become a victim of bullying.

Thus, building a child's self-esteem has been a constant theme of her work, both as a headteacher and as a researcher and author.

It is no coincidence, therefore, that visitors to her schools always commented on how confident the children were. She was often asked how this confidence could be developed. On retiring from headship, she responded to requests to 'bottle' this knowledge and to make it available to parents worldwide.

This workbook therefore offers parents the benefits of her expertise in how to develop children's self-confidence. It is underpinned by the findings of empirical studies, and presents research-driven, practical solutions for developing and strengthening children's strategies for protecting themselves from the effects of bullying.

Table of Contents

1.Introduction

As a parent, I know what it's like to have a child desperate not to go to school in the morning, and I know the gut-wrenching feeling, the physical pain of leaving a child at the school gates, when you suspect that they might be suffering at the hand of others. As a headteacher, I also know from first-hand what it's like to be on the receiving end of parents' distress – parents whose families are being destroyed by the pain of watching their children suffer.

Being able to handle bullies is an essential life skill.

The thought that your child might be a victim to bullies is every parent's nightmare. Bullying surveys such as the latest National Bullying Survey [1] paint a grim picture. On the one hand, they report worrying statistics about the extent of a wide range of bullying activities. On the other hand, they say that teachers feel helpless to do anything about the problem. For instance, they suggest that more than 50% of children have taken time off school because of bullying, whilst at the same time they report that teachers feel that despite any amount of sympathy and good will on their part, they are powerless to impose effective sanctions on bullying behaviour.

Anti-bullying initiatives have come and gone. Huge amounts of charity and tax payers' money has gone into programmes such as Beat Bullying (at time of press it is liquidated), Kidscape [2], Bullying UK [3] and Kids Company (at time of press also in liquidation).

However, the essential point I make in this book, is that, despite the millions of pounds which have been ploughed into anti-bullying initiatives, despite the grand gestures of the tremendously well-meaning celebrities who endorse these initiatives, despite the myriad of self-help groups, those who wear wristbands (how does that help?), the forums and Facebook pages, and despite the grand

9

words of the government, schools and authorities, *bullying is not going away*. At all. In fact, it is getting worse [4].

[At this stage, it is important to separate the one-on-one person-to-person bullying, from the modern scourge of cyberbullying (bullying via electronic communication tools), because they arise from slightly different psychological perspectives, but needless to say, both aspects of bullying have seen an increase over the past decade, with cyberbullying seeing the steepest rise [5].]

It's my contention that bullying is an unfortunate aspect of human nature – and that the rise of the internet has facilitated the primeval urge that insecure individuals feel to dominate and prevail over other human beings. This need to survive and to predominate over other humans should logically have lessened with the progress of civilisation, but the anonymity of the internet has enabled a tsunami of cyberbullying, in the form of *trolling, flaming, impersonation, stalking, outing* and other such horrors [6] which seem to surface all too frequently. The rise in cyberbullying has also coincided with a rise in 'conventional' bullying. Perhaps it is no coincidence, and the one has fuelled the other. Whatever the cause, the outcome is indisputable – bullying is on the rise.

We, as parents, may feel that we can shield our children from this problem by limiting access to the technology which facilitates it (laptops, tables, smart phones – and yes, gaming consoles [7]).

But here is my point: some of us tend to be bullied – and others not. What separates us and them? How can we make sure that we are in the 'never bullied' group, rather than the 'victim' group? For this we need to explore the psychology of the bully and the psychology of the victim, which I shall do in Chapter Three.

This workbook gathers together a range of tried and tested techniques which have been found most useful in helping parents to a) protect their children from bullies and b) implement anti-bullying strategies if the need arises.

I shall try not to get too technical. (It is, after all, a workbook for parents, and not a doctoral thesis). But where necessary, I shall quote the research which has underpinned the ideas being proposed.

Chapter Two: *Signs and Indicators of Bullying* includes a series of simple checklists, to help you to determine whether or not your child is being bullied. The more ticks in the boxes, the more likely it is that they are suffering bullying. This chapter also details the different aspects of bullying, and its effects.

Chapter Three: *The Psychology of Bullying* is an important chapter because it explores the psychology of the bully and the psychology of the victim. Why is it important to know this? Because it provides the *evidence* for the conclusion that both bullying and victimhood stem from insecurity, and insecurity stems from low self-esteem.

Its conclusion drives home **one single point** – *that to protect your child from bullies, you need to address and build their self-esteem.*

The rest of the workbook tells you how to do that.

Chapter Four: *Building Self-esteem* focuses on developing the self-esteem of children from infant to teenager. The chapter draws on the research of many others, and in so doing it will refer to you their works in case you wish to read further.

If you are lucky enough to have obtained this workbook whilst your child is still very young, then it is important to focus upon Chapter Four. *Building Self-esteem*. If you are not so lucky, and if your child has already experienced bullying, then your focus should be on both Chapter Four: *Building Self-esteem* and Chapter Five: *Anti-bullying Strategies* - which offers advice for children, teens at school and teenagers online.

Chapter Six offers a workbooks of exercises which enables you and your child to practise the strategies offered in the book.

The sad fact is that bullying is an activity that has always been – and always will be. Human nature is cruel, and despite decades of attempts to eradicate bullying, it is as rife as ever. It isn't within the power of the individual to change society, but it is within our power to make small changes which will reduce the chances of our children featuring on the bullies' radar.

This workbook will attempt to show you how. It draws upon my 45 years of experience as a teacher, headteacher, school inspector, friend, carer, researcher, parent and grandparent. Ideas offered are based upon the research-based conclusion that the way to support a child who is being bullied is to find out why it is happening to them, to strengthen their self-belief and self-esteem, to give them an armoury of anti-bully skills and strategies and to regard the maintenance of high self-esteem as an essential skill which will serve them throughout their life. Time spent on these strategies will be repaid a thousand-fold – in school, in relationships and in the workplace.

The approach of this book complements and supports the initiatives put forward by government and charity organisations, but it differs fundamentally in one significant aspect. Whereas in all major anti-bullying initiatives the answer has been for the victim to 'tell someone' (has that worked for your child?) the solution offered in this book goes much further and gets to the heart of why a child is bullied in the first place. It then seeks to redress the imbalance of power between the bully and the victim by focusing on the victim's self-esteem and inner strength, so that they don't appear on the bully's radar.

Finally, the book offers the victim a stock of techniques to deflect the bully's advances. These are techniques which will remain with the child as they grow up and will become invaluable strategies to cope with bullying in the workplace, in relationships and within peer groups.

Notes on Chapter One

....

....

....

....

....

....

....

....

....

....

....

....

....

....

....

....

....

....

....

2: Signs and Indicators of Bullying

2.1: What is bullying?

Dictionary definition: 'A bully is someone who uses strength or power to hurt or frighten other people'. There are several types of bullying:

> **Physical:** including physical harm, kicking, pushing, threatening with weapons, using weapons, hazing (initiation ceremonies, giving the bumps, birthday beatings etc.), having possessions thrown around. This is used by the bully who uses their strength to hurt people and is the form most common to male bullies.

> **Verbal:** name calling, teasing, using cruel nicknames, racist or sexist comments.

> **Criminal:** extortion, physical assault, stealing, cyber bullying (mobile phone, email, malicious blogging and instant messaging).

> **Emotional:** the insidious kind, including rumour-mongering, manipulation, isolation, ignoring, arguing into submission, the silent treatment, giving the 'evils', having possessions stolen or moved, etc. This is used by the bully who uses power to frighten people and is the form most commonly, but not exclusively, used by female bullies.

Physical bullying is, in a way, easier to deal with. There is tangible evidence of what has been done and the required action is fairly clear. The bully has to be either reported or caught red-handed. Either way, there is clear evidence of what has been going on and the school's anti-bullying policy can and should be put into effect – or indeed there may be reason to involve the police. Most overt bullying, including stealing, physical assault, graffiti, extortion, abusive phone calls and mobile phone abuse, is against the law.

If bullying happens in school, it is the *duty* of the school to sort it out and to do so quickly, and if you find yourself in the unfortunate position of needing to contact a school because of a bullying incident, then there are some useful templates for you in the Appendix.

Verbal and emotional bullying is often even more worrying for many children and for their parents. The bully's aim is to demoralise so that they can exert their power over the victim. The most sensitive children can easily fall victim to this kind of bullying because they are vulnerable targets.

Victims of emotional bullying may find it tough to talk about their experiences. They may be paralysed with fear, or just accustomed to keeping their worries to themselves. In this case, it is usually one individual's word against another's; it is very difficult to catch the perpetrator red-handed and it is most likely that the victim will be told to 'get over it', 'find somewhere else to play', or 'stop telling tales'.

Often the bully will call their 'rights' into play, but will afford the victim none. Bullies will often use tears as a way to gain sympathy and the authorities are often confused by the bully into believing that they are in fact the victims. Teachers often find this sort of situation subtle and so difficult to deal with that they are rendered helpless.

If this happens – and it happens a lot – the victim can learn that adults can't help them anyway.

Most anti-bullying initiatives focus on 'telling someone' as the solution to the problem of bullying, as if telling someone will make it go away. As all parents of bullying victims know, this isn't enough. What is needed is action by the person who has been told and if this doesn't happen, as seems to be the case far too often, then the victim is left vulnerable, alone and disillusioned.

Teasing

There is a difference between teasing and bullying. The key word is 'persistent'. Teasing is bullying if it is persistent. Many teachers will find it difficult to sort out a bullying situation if it appears to be just a case of 'teasing'. Parents too may be tempted to tell the child to 'just get over it' because it's necessary to be able to cope with teasing - it's all part of our western style of humour after all.

Teasing happens in a good-humoured way. It is usually done by someone who knows the child well and probably cares for them. Usually, the child will find it funny too – even if they don't, they usually get over it quickly.

Someone who is teased is often able to tease back. However, teasing becomes bullying if it causes distress and if it is persistent in spite of the distress it is causing.

If teasing is done as a means of hurting someone, then it has become bullying.

Key Points to note:

- The child who is most likely to be bullied is one who is very sensitive.
- In general, a child who is bullied feels like a victim and believes that they have been the target of a hurtful act.
- Most bullies do it out of a need for power over others. Some just don't realise that their actions are hurtful to others – they are just very insensitive.
- Some bullies see their actions as a game, focusing on the victim's fear.
- Boys' and girls' peer groups are very different and give rise to different types of gender-specific bullying.
- Bullies are people who **persistently** tease, scare, threaten or physically hurt others who are not as strong as they are.
- Bullying occurs everywhere, not only in the playground.

2.2: Indicators

Bullying is usually defined in terms of it being *unwanted, habitual, intentional and aggressive* behaviour which involves a real or perceived *power imbalance*[8]. It can focus on children, disability, ethnicity, race, gender or sexuality.

How do you know if your child is being bullied? You might think that they would just tell you, but unfortunately this is not the case. Studies have shown that in a surprisingly large proportion of cases, it is often the parents who are the last ones to know [9].

This chapter offers a series of checklists to help parents. If you are ticking more than 50% of the boxes, then your child might be being bullied, and you'll need to ask some careful questions.

Most of us have experienced bullying at some time or another. Recent surveys show that bullying is so prevalent in our society that most of us have been affected by it somehow. We know the feelings of hurt, isolation and fear, of being controlled and subject to the apparent power of another. We may not find it so easy to spot the signs of being bullied in our own children. Indeed, bullying is sometimes so subtle, that your child might not even realise that what they are suffering is actually bullying. They might also, for one reason or another, be very good at hiding their feelings.

The first sign is usually that the child doesn't want to go to school. Some other pointers can be:

2.2.1: Physical signs

- unexplained injuries; e.g., cuts, bruises, torn clothing
- making excuses for those injuries
- lost or destroyed personal possessions
- making excuses for having lost or broken those possessions

17

- regularly losing lunch or pocket money
- money going missing from purses/wallets at home
- frequent headache or stomach aches, feeling sick or feigning illness, particularly at breakfast time
- uncharacteristic change in eating habits, such as over-eating or being unusually hungry; or going off their food
- bedwetting
- self-destructive behaviours such as running away from home, harming themselves, or talking about suicide.

2.2.2: Emotional signs

- feelings of helplessness or decreased self esteem
- anxiety, insecurity, insomnia, nightmares
- becoming uncharacteristically moody or short-tempered
- becoming quiet, withdrawn and uncommunicative
- showing a lack of respect for others.

2.2.3: School-related signs

- reluctance to go to school
- deteriorating grades
- loss of interest in schoolwork
- sudden avoidance of friends
- avoiding social situations such as parties, sleepovers
- having difficulty concentrating
- attempting to stay near or with a teacher or other adult during breaks
- expressions of violence in writings or drawings.

2.2.4: Why is it so difficult to tell?

You may wonder why you have to look for such signs? Why does your child not simply tell you that they are being bullied? Recent studies [10] have determined that fewer than half of victims tell an adult, the reason for this being:

- The victim is generally scared of the bully, and scared of the recriminations that may arise as a result of 'telling' on them. (This is potentially why 'telling someone' isn't necessarily the answer – and why the 'tell someone' strategy hasn't worked, and will continue not to work).
- The victim doesn't realise that what is happening to them is bullying
- The victim may think that they won't be believed.
- The victim may be depressed.
- Bullying is all about power [11], and when an individual is being bullied, they feel helpless and weak [12]. Revealing that weakness feeds into the downward spiral of low self-esteem.
- That power also manifests itself in the victim having a sense of not being in control. The feeling of loss of control is a very confusing emotion, and the victim may feel that telling someone else erodes that sense of control even further.
- Children who are bullied often feel that they are suffering alone, and that parents would not understand how they feel.
- Being bullied is a humiliating experience - one which erodes self-esteem. Bullied children may not want to reveal that humiliation to their parents, for fear that they might upset them, for fear that they may end up being punished (or rejected) for being too weak, or for fear that their parents will encourage them to 'toughen up'

- The victim may fear that their parent may take reprisals on the bully, and thus get them into trouble.

Disturbingly, studies have established that a victim's fear about the dangers of 'telling someone' may even be justified:

> 'When teachers knew about the bullying, they often tried to stop it, but in many cases the bullying stayed the same or even got worse' [13].

Indeed, the same study showed that even when they are told, parents and teachers often neglect to try to do something about the bullying anyway:

> 'With regard to active bullying, neither the majority of the teachers nor parents talked to the bullies about their behaviour.'

2.3: The effects of bullying

Undoubtedly, bullying is damaging to children. Not only can they be physically affected, but it can also affect them socially, emotionally and intellectually. School bullying is responsible for such a high level of unhappiness that for many children, their whole lives are subsequently affected.

The statistics, the latest of which can be found by searching for 'effects of bullying' are horrible. At time of press, statistics ranging from the NSPCC to official government bullying prevention sites report that bullying is responsible for academic problems; school truancy; moving school; dropping out of school altogether and opting for home-schooling; risk of sleep difficulties; anxiety; depression; substance use; violent behaviour; mental health problems; and even suicide.

Children who suffer bullying on a long-term basis can develop feelings of powerlessness and hopelessness. They are also more likely to develop psychological illnesses later on. If they do not tell anyone about the bullying, then they also suffer the extra stress of not receiving support and understanding. Children who become victims of bullying are more likely to have their relationships and their careers affected by victimisation too.

Bullying affects whole families. Children who are victimised may find that the pattern is repeated when they become adults.

Unfortunately, research has shown that victims of bullying can become bullies themselves in later life.

Clearly that undesirable vicious circle is an unthinkable prospect for our own children.

2.4: Notes on Chapter Two

....

....

....

....

....

....

....

....

....

....

....

....

....

....

....

....

....

....

....

....

....

3: The psychology of bullying

3.1: Us and them

Bullying takes place when there is an imbalance of power between the victim and the aggressor [14].

We think of bullies as 'them', but recent studies have shown that a significant proportion of children and young people have engaged in activity which many of us would consider to be bullying. For instance, in the Annual Bullying Survey of 2016 [15] an alarming proportion of the participants (33%) admitted to having purposely upset someone; 20% had actually attacked someone; 19% had excluded someone from a social group; 27% had said something 'nasty' to someone online; 9% had taken or damaged someone else's property, in order to upset them; and 13% had started a rumour about someone. Very interestingly, the vast majority of participants (86%) said that they had 'never bullied' anyone.

It should be noted that this was not a survey of bullies. It was conducted on a broad range of teenagers, from a representative cross-section of ethnicities, religions, gender, household incomes, disabilities, across all areas of the UK.

Clearly the two groups of those who consider themselves bullies and those who consider themselves as victims are not mutually exclusive. Indeed, psychologists caution against *labelling* children as either a 'bully' or a 'victim'. Labelling suggests that behaviours cannot change, and we run the risk of ignoring the fact that children can adopt both roles at different times, and in different situations. That is even aside from all of the other roles played in bullying scenarios (the bystander who provides an audience for the bully; the assister who cheers them on and occasionally joins in; the reinforcer who encourages the bully to carry on etc).

It appears that bullying seems to be part of human nature that many of us have been unable to escape. Research has, unsurprisingly, *overwhelmingly* determined that if you have been bullied, then you are more likely to bully someone else.

Why are some children bullied and others not? Is there such a thing as a 'natural victim'? If your child falls prey to the bullies, what can you do to stop this? To find the answer we have to look at the psychology of bullying.

The research on the subject presents grim reading. The statistics are frightening, but the conclusion is clear:

'Research has overwhelming determined that being bullied is associated with low self-esteem' [16].

Many studies have come to this conclusion [17] [18].

It is clear that we need to be alert to the dangers of being bullied. Studies have determined that both children who bully and those who are bullied are prone to negative feelings – even depressive symptoms and suicidal thoughts - with girls suffering these symptoms more than boys, and with those who are bullied suffering more than those who bully [19] [20].

The process is also a vicious circle - the more frequently children are victimised and/or the more they bully others, the lower their self-esteem. These charts tell the story. These are the self-esteem scores of bullying 'VICTIMS' [21]:

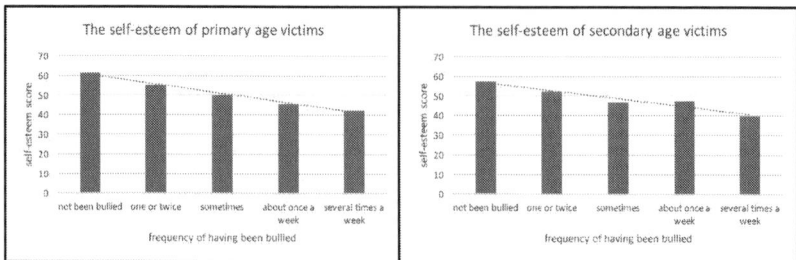

Note that the trend-line is downwards for both age groups – the more they are bullied, the lower the self-esteem.

Then we have the BULLIES:

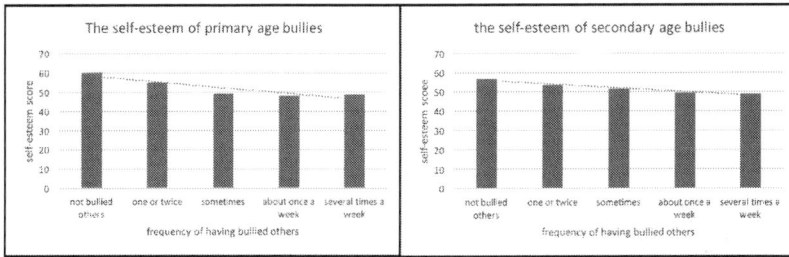

The trend-lines are also downwards, telling us that the more an individual bullies, the lower their own self-esteem.

The researchers who conducted that particular study concluded that **high self-esteem protects** from involvement in bullying:

Thus, in view of the strong relationship between self-esteem and bullying that has been found in the present paper, it is recommended that top priority be given by parents and teachers to preventing and reducing feelings of poor self-worth among children and adolescents'. [22]

If your child has a powerful sense of their self-worth, they will know that they can handle anything and thus they will have nothing to fear.

Bullies are generally cowards who will not pick on someone with a high level of self-esteem. They need to control and dominate, often because of a deficit in their own social skills, and certainly (as we can see above) in tandem with their own low self-esteem. But in order to control someone they need to find a ready victim. The bully does not have any power of their own - the bully's power is centred within the mind of the victim, with the victim being too intimidated to put up effective resistance. This is why the solution to the problem lies within the victims themselves.

I should emphasise here, that this is not a book all about those who bully. The psychology of why an individual engages in bullying behaviour is for another time. Whilst there is an occasional insight into the behaviour of one who bullies, this book focuses rather on those who are bullied – and how parents can protect their children from such behaviour.

3.2: Bullying and gender

Boys tend to be active bullies more often than girls, but whereas boys tend to bully in a more direct way (physical hitting, issuing threats, tripping up, taking and/or destroying things etc.), girls often bully in a more indirect way (psychological bullying, social exclusion, friendship manipulation, name-calling, starting rumours etc.) [23] [24]

Other types of bullying are common to both genders: stealing, teasing, blackmail, intimidation, provoking and annoying [25].

Cyberbullying in the form of flaming and trolling tends to be the province of boys, whereas online rumour-spreading is more prevalent amongst girls. The majority of cyber victims are females, whilst the majority of cyber bullies are males. Also, the majority of cyberbullying victims, of whatever gender, as well as bystanders, do not report incidents to adults [26].

Parents of secondary age children, also report an insidious form of bullying, often perpetrated by girls, which has become known as 'social bullying'. This is 'socially acceptable behaviour, as in a highly competitive approach to academic, sporting or social success, which, by intent, makes others feel inferior or causes distress' [27].

However, taking all types of bullying together, most studies have established that there is no difference in numbers between girls and boys when it comes to being a victim of bullying: boys are just as likely to be bullied as girls (although girls *suffer* more as a consequence). These are generalisations of course, but they are nevertheless supported by rafts of research findings.

3.3: Why might your child be bullied?

This section can be painful, but you need to understand why your own child is a target for bullies. You may choose the path of blame and believe that your child was simply 'in the wrong place at the wrong time'. If the attack has only happened once, then this is probably the case. But if the bullying is **persistent**, and if your child is targeted, then you need to consider why this is happening.

Does your child make it easy for the bully? Bullies tend to pick on younger, smaller, weaker or more sensitive children, but they are also doing it to aggrandise their own sense of power, and they will continue only if they are getting a result.

Bullies tend to have a go at a lot of children, before focusing on those who will react quickly and who will 'reward' the bullying with a reaction. They also tend to be cowards and will quickly move on to a more likely victim if they do not get a reaction.

These are some of the reasons why children are bullied. Check to see which ones may be relevant to your child. Add your own reasons.

- Wrong place at the wrong time
- Under-developed for their age
- Physically different
- Different race/culture
- Has learning difficulties
- Over-protected
- Is particularly talented
- Family problems
- Over-sensitive
- Shy
- Tends to provoke
- Recently joined the group

- Low self-esteem
- Wears glasses, braces etc.
- Unusual habits, stutter etc.
- Unusual name

Our own reasons:

....

....

....

The odd one out in that list is 'wrong place at the wrong time'. If a child is attacked in a one-off incident, even if the attack comes from a known bully, then the incident is more of an assault than a bullying incident. An assault needs to be reported immediately, if necessary to the police, and you can expect that it will be dealt with appropriately.

The key to recognising bullying is that it is a *persistent* offence. The reason why the bully continues to upset your child is because it works.

In order to prevent your child from being bullied, you should strengthen:

- their self-esteem (Chapter Four)
- their anti-bullying strategies (Chapter Five)

3.4: Does the victim help the bully?

This may seem like a very strange question, but the truth is that many bullying victims assist the bully by reinforcing the behaviour that the bully is expecting.

The child will be feeding the bully's sense of power if they:

- avoid making eye contact
- blush easily
- show that they are upset
- over-react
- display submissive reactions
- blame themselves

A child with low self-esteem is likely to be *inviting* the bully to disrespect them. Furthermore, by *reacting*, they are giving the bully exactly what they want.

The bully will soon work out which taunts are going to get a reaction and which not.

If your child is bullied, then it is possible that they have low self-esteem.

The way they are treated by other children is a reflection of how they feel about themselves.

3.5: Notes on Chapter Three

....

....

....

....

....

....

....

....

....

....

....

....

....

....

....

....

....

....

....

....

....

....

....

....

4: Building self-esteem

Schools tend to use a strategy of encouraging students to report bullying, so that remedial action can be focused upon the bully. However, if you attempt to stop bullying by focusing on the bully, then another one will just fill the place as soon as they are gone.

Of course, bullies need to be reported and brought to account for their actions – school anti-bullying policies detail this approach very clearly, and all anti-bullying strategies and initiatives make it their mission to eradicate bullying by getting rid of the bully.

But has it worked for your child? Is it getting any better?

According to research, 'The impact of the introduction of policies on bullying throughout a school seems to be limited' [28]. The evidence is that a child who is bullied by one is likely to be bullied by another [29].

The secret is not to become a victim in the first place.

As determined in Chapter Three, the way to protect your child from bullies is to focus on building their self-esteem and their anti-bullying strategies.

The first thing we shall do is to check your child's level of self-esteem.

4.1: Checking self-esteem

Your child is special – a worthy and lovable being who deserves the best. They have the right to wake up happily each morning, knowing that they are safe and that they can face the day with optimism, looking forward to the rewards and challenges of the day.

The following checklists will help you to put into perspective your child's current level of self-esteem. (NB. Never confuse self-esteem with arrogance. Arrogance is an over-evaluation of your worth, while high self-esteem is having a healthy opinion of yourself.)

This is an activity for parent and child together.

Read through this list, saying the words *'I am'* before each of them and score as follows: Almost Never (0); Sometimes (1); Often (2); Almost Always (3):

adventurous ( ) kind ( ) interesting ( ) happy ( ) depressed ( )

shy ( ) loveable ( ) lazy ( ) intelligent ( ) trustworthy ( ) funny ( )

optimistic ( ) negative ( ) proud ( ) positive ( ) embarrassed ( )

energetic ( ) guilty ( ) boring ( ) self-conscious ( ) demanding ( )

bullied ( ) in control ( ) stupid ( ) helpless ( ) fearful ( ) sad ( )

confident ( ).

How did they score?

Words which scored a 3:

. . . .

Words which scored a 0:

. . . .

Analysing the scores

Look at the list of all the words which scored a 3. This is what your child thinks they are always. What does this reveal about their self-image? Does it mean that they have high or low self-esteem? Would you and they like to change any of these?

Highlight the ones you would *both* like to change. Which words do you need to increase from a score of 0 to a score of 3? Write them here:

. . . .

There were some positive and some negative words in this list.

The next stage of this exercise will reinforce only the positive.

Go through the following checklist with your child and agree together which words describe them. You will be surprised at how many you can tick. Add some more positive words of your own:

lovable ( ) loyal ( ) sensible ( ) kind ( ) loving ( ) friendly ( )

gentle ( ) generous ( ) funny ( ) free ( ) truthful ( ) talented ( )

careful ( ) thoughtful ( ) curious ( ) patient ( ) trusting ( )

creative ( ) capable ( ) sensitive ( ) playful ( ) determined ( )

tidy ( ) calm ( ) full of energy ( ) positive ( ) cooperative ( )

excited ( ) honest ( ) interested ( ) healthy ( ) joyful ( )

organised ( ) polite ( ) practical ( ) sense of humour ( )

. . . .( ) . . . .( ) . . . .( )

Now highlight any words which you would *both like* to describe your child but which don't at the moment.

What did you find out?

You should now have an idea of:

- Your child's level of self-esteem
- What they like about themselves (this is a very relevant starter)
- What qualities they would like to add to their portfolio of self-worth

You may have discovered now that they have some beliefs about themselves which you feel need to be changed.

After looking at the results of the last exercise, write down those beliefs that your child has about themselves, which you both feel need to be changed:

....

....

....

....

....

....

....

....

....

....

....

....

....

Children with high self-esteem are:

- Able to accept and learn from their own mistakes
- Confident without being arrogant or conceited
- Not demoralised by criticism or mild teasing
- Able to deal with their own feelings
- Less likely to be defensive when questioned
- Not easily upset by setbacks, obstacles, failures or looking foolish
- Unlikely to feel a need to put others down
- Assertive but not aggressive in communicating their needs
- More likely to resist peer pressure
- Able to bounce back from disappointments and failures
- Not self-critical
- Not needing to prove themselves
- Able to take responsibility for their own happiness
- Able to laugh at themselves, not taking themselves too seriously
- Accepting of themselves as they are
- Able to cope with change
- Generous to themselves, as well as others
- Able to accept generosity and compliments
- Able to use assertive language, using statements beginning with 'I'
- Able to say 'No', without offending the other person
- Able to set goals for themselves and strive to reach them.

How many of the above do you need to work on with your child?

Bullies avoid people with a strong sense of character, those who exude a powerful sense of self-worth. Children with high self-esteem will not feed the bully's need for power. Strengthen your child's self-esteem and the bullies will move on somewhere else.

4.1.1. Ideas which we need to follow up:

....

....

....

....

....

....

....

....

....

....

....

....

....

....

....

....

....

....

....

....

....

4.2: Self-esteem techniques

4.2.1: Affirmations

Psychological studies have demonstrated the effectiveness of the use of 'positive affirmations' to support and raise the self-esteem of individuals of all ages [30] [31]. It is a neuro-linguistic technique which re-trains the internal monologue (self-chatter) that goes on constantly in the mind.

The general idea is that we become what we think we are, and that if we re-train our thinking and talking patterns, then our sub-conscious gradually assimilates positive messages and consequently acts upon our self-esteem.

'As you think, so shall you be' (Our thoughts create our experiences)

Affirmations have long been accepted as a very powerful tool for changing entrenched thought patterns in adults. Children learn to use them even more quickly and easily. They enjoy pattern and repetition.

The key to making the affirmations work is **repetition: so much so that you persuade your subconscious mind that they are true. By continually bombarding your subconscious with these statements, you are re-programming your mind in the most powerful way**.

Affirmations:

- Are written in the present tense (I am…)
- State a deliberate intention (I feel happier all the time)
- Must not admit defeat (This probably won't work)
- Must not be conditional (If I succeed then ….)
- Must not be about anybody other than you
- Must be spoken out loud and written down
- Must be repeated time and time again.

Each time you teach your child an affirmation, make sure that they are repeating it with you. The more often you both say it, the more effective it will be in empowering both of you. They will feel double the benefit. As you read the affirmation, point out the writing on the pages. This double input will increase the effectiveness even further.

How do we choose which ones to use?

In the section of this book on 'checking self-esteem', you came up with a set of characteristics which you prioritised as being important to change in your child. This section helps you to help your child to make that change. Just say that you identified that your child scored low on 'optimism'.

Choose the most appropriate affirmation from the list, or make one up of your own:

- There are many things I do successfully (think of all those things you have already written down)
- I don't have to be perfect to approve of myself
- I continue to feel strong and secure inside
- I love my family and accept them as they are
- I am responsible for the decisions I make
- I am achieving my goals and ambitions
- I am a unique individual
- I find it easy to make new friends
- I am lovable
- I speak clearly and confidently
- The ideas in this book have worked for other children, so I will give them a try myself
- My self-belief grows stronger all the time
- I stay calm
- I learn quickly and easily
- I like to help others

- I'm a good person
- I finish what I start
- Every mistake I make is an opportunity to learn
- I deserve support and will ask for help when I need it
- I live life with courage and confidence
- I will treat myself as someone special
- I decide what success means to me
- I feel happier all the time
- I can achieve many great things
- Challenges are exciting
- I am comfortable with who I am
- I learn new things easily
- I am developing the habit of positive thinking
- The way to make friends is to be friendly
- I don't need to play with children who are unfair
- I don't have to put up with bullying
- The world is a beautiful place
- I deserve the best
- I am strong enough to go and find something interesting to do elsewhere
- I do not rely on the good opinion of others.

Try to work on just one aspect of self-esteem per week (i.e., one affirmation).

Write an *Affirmation of the Week* on a number of sticky notes and paste them around your child's room and around the rest of the house. Get your child to draw frames around them and decorate them, using symbols which relate to other interests in their life.

Another good idea is to have them move across the screen on the computer screensaver.

Adapt the affirmation to suit your child's circumstances, but make sure that you keep it in the present tense, as if you are currently achieving it with a definite intention for the future.

Write it down in a diary or journal each day for a week. At the end of the week, create a new affirmation.

Assessing the effectiveness of the affirmation

To assess how effective any particular affirmation is, you just have to score it out of ten at the beginning and again at the end of the week:

Before: How much do I believe that this describes me? (/10)

Affirmation:

....

After: How much do I believe that this describes me? (/10)

An important note about self-belief:

If you think that no-one will like you,

then that is exactly what you will get.

If you think that everyone likes you,

then that is exactly what you will get.

Notes on affirmations:

....

....

....

....

....

Creeds

A creed is an affirmation technique which supports the construction of an inner belief system. You are writing down what you believe that you are. A good place to start is to borrow lines from famous books or poems – lines which describe you as a person (e.g., Winnie the Pooh).

Make sure that your creed is all written in positive language and that it is stated in the present tense with a future intention, e.g., 'I believe that I am getting more confident every day'.

Of course, the secret, as with the rest of the suggestions in this book, is to *practise* what you have written, by saying your creed to yourself every day.

The difference between an affirmation and a creed is that an affirmation is what you *want*, whereas a creed is what you already *are:*

I believe that I

....

....

I believe that I

....

....

I believe that I

....

....

Some suggestions for key words that your child might include in their creed: courageous; take responsibility; kind; generous; strong; freedom. (Hint: look at section 4.2 for ideas.)

4.3: Mindset

There is a considerable body of research, led by Professor Carol Dweck at Stanford University, around the notion of *'fixed vs growth mindset'* [32]. Her very important and well-respected research has established that success is more related to a positive mindset than innate ability.

She claims that praising a child for the sake of it, is detrimental.

According to her findings, the way to support a child's self-confidence is to avoid praising them for their *intelligence*, and rather to praise them for their *effort*. If a child is told they are clever – why would they need to put in any effort?

> *'Emphasizing effort gives a child a variable that they can control. They come to see themselves as in control of their success. Emphasizing natural intelligence takes it out of the child's control, and it provides no good recipe for responding to a failure.'* [33]

How does this relate to a child's self-esteem? The answer is that success, gained through effort, breeds further success – and success feeds self-esteem.

Her very compelling work is well worth a read.

Putting her ideas into practice:

- Praise them for their effort, in front of other people: 'Well done – you must have worked hard on that.' (Not, well done – you are clever.')
- Leave messages for them where they can find them privately.
- Make sure that the last thing they hear at night is a positive affirmation of something they have achieved through hard work.
- Write a list together, in their journal, of all achievements that have been achieved through hard work.

- Let grandparents and other relatives know the strategy – and get them to reinforce the notion that success comes through hard work.
- Sincerity of praise is most important – make sure that praise is *specific and focused*, not general. Children are very good at detecting a hidden agenda.

You can help your child to build their self-esteem by changing their internal monologue from a *fixed mindset* to a *growth mindset* [32]:

Fixed Mindset: I don't think I can do it because I don't have the talent.

Growth Mindset: Perhaps I can't do it now, but I may be able to, if I put in the time and effort.

Fixed Mindset: If I fail, then I'll be called a failure.

Growth Mindset: Every successful person had lots of failures on the way. If they hadn't failed, they wouldn't have eventually succeeded.

Fixed Mindset: If I don't try, then no one will know that I can't do it.

Growth Mindset: If I don't try then I won't give myself a chance to succeed.

There is an exercise on this in Chapter Six of this book, but here is a space for you to add your own:

Fixed Mindset ....

....

Growth Mindset ....

....

4.3.1: How to change our self-beliefs

One of the ways we can change our beliefs is to change the language we use to describe ourselves. Instead of using destructive self-talk, we can re-phrase our statements in a positive way. This instructs our subconscious to re-frame our view of ourselves.

Children understand this concept really easily if it is played as a game, with these as examples:

Existing 'faulty' belief: I am different from others and people don't like me.

New positive belief: I am glad that I am different and that makes me very lovable.

Existing 'faulty' belief: I deserve to be bullied because I am no good at anything.

New positive belief: I understand why I have been bullied, but that's going to stop now.

Existing 'faulty' belief: Nobody will ever stop the bullying.

New positive belief: The ideas in this book have worked for other children, and they can work for me too.

There is an exercise like this in Chapter Six, but here is a space for you to add your own in the meantime:

'Faulty' belief ....

....

....

Positive belief ....

....

....

4.4: Family activities: doing things together

Without a doubt, the most effective way of improving your child's self-esteem is to spend time with them and to look for opportunities to praise their achievements. It could be whilst you are doing the cooking together, fixing something in the garage or pulling up the onions in the allotment.

This also gives you every opportunity to provide a role model, showing them how you look after yourself, respect and treat yourself. At this time, you can make sure that they know that you like them, that you admire their qualities and that you value their presence in the family.

4.4.1: Catch them doing something well

This is a favourite amongst teachers, for changing negative behaviour into positive:

Find every opportunity to tell your child that they are doing well. Reinforce their self-esteem by giving them positive feedback wherever possible.

Examples:

- 'Your writing is getting better and better all the time. You must be working hard at it'
- 'Well done for tidying your room – you really are getting better at it.'
- 'Wow – I didn't know you could do that! When did you learn to do that?'
- 'You were really kind to Jimmy. I bet that made them feel really good.'

4.4.2: Play empathy games

There is a genre of board games which develops empathy [34] and family harmony, rather than individual competitiveness. They include:

- *Pandemic*
- *Forbidden Island*
- *Forbidden Desert*

If you want to play an excellent competitive board game (which only lasts half an hour), then try *Carcassonne*.

4.4.3: Other ways we can do things together as a family

....

....

....

....

....

....

....

....

....

....

....

....

....

....

4.5: How to be happy

This is a family activity, whereby you choose the best 'tips' for your child. You can work on as many as you like at once.

For children from primary age upwards:

- As you put your head on your pillow at night, look forward to the next few minutes of thinking of all the best things that could possibly happen to you. No-one can spoil this moment, because it is private and only you know about it.
- Wear strongly coloured clothes.
- When you find an unhappy or negative thought creeping into your head, say 'OUT!', drop it like a football onto your foot - and boot it out into space. You may like to go somewhere private and actually act it out.
- Expect the BEST to happen to you and it will happen. (By the way, if you expect the WORST – that will happen too). Your subconscious is so powerful that what it expects will happen, will usually do so. If you expect happiness, then you will attract happiness.
- Smile at people – see the result.
- At night time, give your worries to a worry-doll who will look after them during the night - you will feel much better in the morning. You can always take your worries back in the morning (but you probably won't want to).
- Ask Mum to give you a massage.

For children from secondary age upwards:

- Be generous with your compliments.
- Take your dog (or someone else's) for a walk. Spend some time stroking a furry animal and feel the softness of its coat.
- Keep fit. Using energy up in physical fitness creates even

more energy. Powerful chemicals are released in your body while you are exercising and for a long time afterwards. They work every time, don't have any after effects and improve your health.

- Have a joke book at hand. Tell a really funny one to your granny, the cat or dog. Have a joke a day to tell your friends. They will seek you out. Everyone likes a friend with a smiley face – you will be very popular.

- Make a habit of telling people only your good news, not the bad news. It will make other people feel happy and they will look forward to seeing you again.

- Don't use up all your energy listening to 'needy' friends. Yes, you understand how they feel, but your mood could be dragged down at a time when you really need it to be boosted up. When people try to tell you their bad news, ask, 'what good things happened to you today?

- 'Life is what happens while you are making other plans,' said John Lennon. Concentrate on the present and don't worry about the past. You can't do anything about the past, no matter how good or bad it was. It's gone. Neither can you affect the future by worrying about it. If anything, worrying will drain your energy and it will not have the slightest effect on what happens.

- If you find yourself criticising another person, then stop and say something constructive and complimentary instead.

- You don't always have to be 'right'. Sometimes it's best just to choose to be 'kind', even though you know the other person is in the wrong.

- Choose an affirmation from your Affirmation List and have fun telling it to yourself ten times every morning and night for a week. Then choose another one.

4.6: Visualisation & goal-setting

From Aristotle 2000 years ago, to advanced techniques used in modern sport psychology, visualisation (the creation of a mental image of a future event), has been acknowledged as a very effective technique for changing an individual's self-belief.

It is a really powerful activity, so it is worth spending some time practising this technique – and, according to lots of anecdotal evidence, it really works.

The secret to success is to really believe that you can achieve. The power of visualisation is that it convinces your subconscious mind that you can.

Having visualised the desired outcome (being a confident individual who does not invite bullying), we begin to see the possibility of achieving the outcome. By visualising, we imagine what our preferred future might be. Once we have 'seen' this future, we then become motivated to achieve it and can set goals towards it.

Below are the general principles of how visualisation and goal-setting work together.

Children are particularly motivated by this activity, which can become an effective life-skill:

1. Note where you are now, your situation and feelings (e.g. being bullied).
2. Decide on your goal (e.g. self-confidence).
3. Write down your goal and draw a picture of it, if possible.
4. Close your eyes and have a clear image of yourself achieving the goal.
5. Imagine yourself as if you have already achieved it.
6. Enjoy the achievement in your imagination. Breathe it, smell it, feel it. Look at the world from your new

perspective.

7. Plan the first step towards your new goal and start straight away.

8. When you wake up each morning, say to yourself, 'What am I going to do today towards achieving my target?' Do one thing each day and your goal will be achieved much earlier than you thought it would.

9. Act as if your goal has already been achieved.

4.6.1: The 'Confidence-Trick'

This is a visualisation exercise, which is designed to change an individual's internal belief system.

Stand in front of a mirror and imagine that your reflection is looking at you **from the future**. The future is a wonderful time, because you have done all of the exercises in this guide; the bullying has stopped; you feel really good about yourself and you have such wonderful self-confidence that people are amazed at how much you have changed.

Now look at the future person and see how they are standing; how their shoulders are square and straight; how they have a confident smile and how tall they are. Take a moment to enjoy being that person.

How do you feel?

What does your body look like?

Enjoy being that person, because it is YOU.

Now, when you have really got into the feeling of that future person, close your eyes and imagine walking into the mirror and morphing and merging straight into your future person. **See the world from the eyes of your future person. Feel what it is like to be your future person.**

Now pinch your fingers together quite hard to 'anchor' the feeling of confidence.

Pinch them harder as you imagine what it is like to be merged into your future confident person.

When you need a bit of confidence, visualise your future person, pinch your thumb and first finger together and remember the good feeling.

Repeat this exercise many times, until the Confidence-Trick gives you a more powerful glow of confidence every time you use it.

4.6.2: The Golden Light of Confidence

This is a wonderful technique which your child can adapt to countless situations in their life.

Make sure that they are in a peaceful space and they are warm, well fed and comfortable.

Put on some restful music which will help them to become calm and relaxed.

Read this to them:

> *Breathe deeply and slowly, trying to slow down your heart-rate. Now close your eyes and imagine that a golden light is pouring down, through the top of your skull and working its way through your entire body. Feel this golden light of* **confidence** *coming down through your spine and out into your limbs. Now imagine that the light is forming a shield around you, a wall of energy and confidence. Whatever the bully says, they can't hurt you. Even more than that, whenever the bully send nasty vibes at you — they get bounced back.*

4.7: Making children feel good about themselves

The first item is the most important – and for some working families it is the most difficult, because of the pressures of balancing work and family life.

- Even if it only once a week, try to eat together if possible. Discuss the day; identify the positives and praise your child for achievement gained through effort.
- Prioritise family leisure time, centered on the child's interests.
- Make sure that your own mood is positive.
- Praise them in front of other people.
- Leave messages for them where they can find them privately.
- Make sure that the last thing they hear at night is a positive affirmation of their qualities, achievements and successes.
- Write a list together of all their qualities – stick it on the fridge.
- Involve your child in family decisions, such as major purchases or family holidays. It will confirm to them that they are valued and important to you.
- Give them responsibilities and praise them for fulfilling them.
- Play board games together and praise them when they win.
- Let grandparents and other relatives know how well they are doing.
- Ask them about the good things that happened at school today.
- Praise them at any time, but especially when you see them behaving in a confident manner.
- Encourage them to take risks. Limit the risks to one at a time and make sure they understand and appreciate their own success. Make them small risks at first, like changing a

routine or trying a different food. Each risk will increase their confidence.

- Allocate regular quality time to discuss what support they need in school or anything else.

4.7.1: The ideas that will work for us as a family:

....

....

....

....

....

....

....

....

....

....

....

....

....

....

....

....

....

....

4.8: How to say 'no'

The capacity to say 'no', is an essential skill for life, and is vital for a child who has the potential to be bullied. Being able to say 'no' strengthens self-confidence. Each time an individual succeeds in saying 'no', it becomes easier the next time.

You might be thinking to yourself that your child already knows rather well how to say, 'no'! But saying 'no' when under pressure from peers is something that many of us find difficult. It is even more difficult for a child who is naturally quiet or shy, especially in the face of a bully who is intent on exerting their power.

The key is to realise that it is our **right** to say 'no' and that it is perfectly acceptable to do so.

Go through this tip with your child and *try to make it into a game*. It is by **practising** these techniques, that they will become part of your child's armoury against a bully. Here goes:

When someone asks you to do something which you don't want to do, look the other person in the eye.

Make sure that the first word you use is 'No'. Say something like:

- No, I am not comfortable with that
- No, I am in the middle of something
- No, I don't enjoy that
- No, I was just about to go and do something else
- No, it wouldn't leave me any time to play
- No, try and find someone else to do it for you

Don't offer to help the other person out; don't say 'sorry'; don't make excuses.

Remember that it is your right to say 'no'.

If all else fails – walk away.

4.9: Keeping a success diary

Research has suggested that a powerful way to improve self-esteem is through keeping a journal [35]. The positive self-talk that we generated in the previous chapter can be reinforced with what we can call a Success Diary. There are some commercial diaries that you can buy, which have headings already suggested for you, but there is nothing as effective as creating your own.

For this diary, your child will need a special book – preferably plain paper – with some appropriate decoration on the cover, which represents your child's interests. You'll also need coloured pencils or pens, stickers etc. This is essentially a journal, but which, for obvious reasons, only records successes. If you put *journaling* into an internet search engine, you will get lots of ideas (but remember only to pick the positive ones).

Using a separate page for each topic, encourage your child to explore such topics as:

- My achievements over the past year
- Aspects of my character that I am proud of
- Things to be happy about
- My Future Self
- Things to be grateful for
- Affirmation of the Day
- A picture of a person who loves me (and in speech bubbles write down what that person would say about you)
- Brain Dump: My brilliant ideas
- Boredom Buster List
- Mum and Me Time List
- Things I like about my friends
- About me page – interests, hobbies, loves.
- Things I am good at
- Yearly Resolutions/Goals

- Learning Goals
- Reading Log (author, genre etc.)
- Books I need to read
- Book reviews
- Savings/ Chores Tracker
- 100 things I want to do with my life
- Places I want to see
- My favourite music
- Favourite Quotes
- Best doodles
- Recipes & meal planner
- Advice (to others, and/or myself)
- What's on my mind
- Art ideas
- Pocket money tracker
- Project Ideas
- My Challenges
- Favourite food
- Gift ideas
- 5 Year Plan
- Spellings I need to learn
- Exciting new vocabulary
- My favourite films
- My homes
- My holidays
- If I knew I could not fail, I would ......
- How to make the next year my Best Year Yet!

This chapter has offered parents a number of ways for them to work together with their child, to build self-esteem, in order to provide a 'bully-shield', and in order to reduce the chances of an individual featuring on a bully's radar.

However, it may be that your child is already the victim of bullies. In which case the next chapter is equally important.

4.10: Notes on Chapter Four

....

....

....

....

....

....

....

....

....

....

....

....

....

....

....

....

5: Anti-bullying strategies

It is no coincidence that strong, resourceful and confident children don't usually become the target of a bully. The last thing a bully wants is to face someone who is emotionally stronger than they are. If a bully suspects that they can intimidate someone, then that is exactly what they will try to do.

The central message of this guide is that children should assume some responsibility for stopping the bullying themselves. This skill will become invaluable to them throughout their lives. Does bullying happen only in schools? What about the workplace – even the family? The strategies and techniques involved in learning how to protect themselves will remain with them throughout their lives and will become essential life-skills.

Indeed, it is our *responsibility* to educate our children in this way. We are doing them no service by protecting them, without giving them the strategies to deal with the 'nasty' as well as the 'nice'. They need to learn how to interact with all of those who would wish to prey upon their vulnerability.

This chapter offers practical advice and activities for those whose children are already suffering from being bullied. In line with the tone of the rest of the workbook, these ideas are for parents to work alongside their children.

The chapter covers:

1. *Body language*
2. *Anti-bullying tricks*
3. *Controlling feelings and emotions*
4. *How to deal with girls' cliques*
5. *Cyberbullying*
6. *Managing school officials*

5.1: Body language

5.1.1: Posture

It is worth spending time working on your child's body language. Their body language will reveal their inner confidence, true feelings and intentions in a way that a hundred words would not. This includes their posture, hand gestures, facial expressions, and eye movements.

If you believe in yourself, it will show in your body language and other people will believe in you too.

The social psychologist Dr Amy Cuddy, in her famous TED Talk [36], claims that 'Your body language shapes who you are'. She advocates 'power posing' – standing in a confident manner, (like Wonder Woman or Batman!) even if you don't feel so confident – as a means of actually boosting self-confidence.

She suggests that we can change other people's perceptions of ourselves – just by paying attention to our body language. Even more than that, she says that repeatedly standing in a confident manner, can actually change our body chemistry and give us confidence in otherwise anxiety-inducing situations.

Translate this to the bully-victim situation, and your child is conjuring self-confidence at the time they need it most.

Considerable research [37] with varying results, has been conducted to verify this powerful claim, but many body language experts agree that it is an effective confidence-boosting technique.

Assertive standing, then, involves standing straight and 'thinking tall', as if an invisible thread is joined to the top of the head and is pulling you upwards. Feet need to be planted firmly on the ground with the body square on, shoulders back, using up as much 'space' as possible. Good posture tells others that you are confident, self-assured and poised.

The bully is less likely to attack a confident looking person.

Matching and mirroring the other's body language (without being a copy-cat) can reduce the tension between two children. For instance, if one child is leaning on a wall, then 'matching' the body language would mean that the other child would be leaning too.

5.1.2: *Eye contact*

Research linked with the Amy Cuddy studies has determined that direct eye gaze also increases self-confidence [38].

Let's see how this idea would translate into three eye contact exercises which develop the confidence of a bully victim:

- Don't even think about it!
- Get the look
- Eye gaze game

Don't even think about it!

Stand or sit facing a mirror, thinking about a time when you have been bullied.

Look at your face. Are your eyes shining and bright, or are you looking down or sideways? Are your lips tight or is your mouth open and smiley?

Look at your shoulders. Are they slumped over or pulled back and straight?

Say 'hello' to yourself (go on – I know it sounds silly). What is your voice like – small, quiet, muffled, grunting – or loud and confident?

Look again at yourself. This is the person that the bully is seeing. Is your body language going to tell the bully that they are likely to succeed in intimidating you? Do you want them to come back again? (I don't think so.)

Now let's change that body language. Imagine that you are strong, invincible. Let's tell that cowardly bully – **'Don't even think about it!'**

Think of a time when you have done something really well, when you have been particularly successful. Perhaps it was a time when your teacher praised you in front of the class and it made you feel really good. Perhaps it was when you learned to swim or ride a bike. Hold that feeling now. What does it feel like? Look at your body language this time. Make sure that you are standing tall – even taller. Are your eyes twinkling? Is there a happy confident smile on your lips? Or a quiet determination perhaps?

Now this is the best bit. Look into the mirror at the bully. Not scared of them now are you? Look hard at them and *think to yourself,* **'Don't even think about it'**.

Now you should *practise* that look and that feeling. **Make the message come out of your eyes.** Tell the mirror, with your eyes and facial expression, 'don't even think about it!' Now make eye contact with the bully, stand tall and walk away.

Do this exercise time and time again, so that your body knows exactly what to do when a bully comes up to you. The bully will recognise instantly that you are different and it will make them uncertain and less brave.

Get the Look

Maintaining eye contact is really important if someone is trying to exert power over you. Not only should you keep eye contact, but you need to remember that your eyes reflect what you are saying 'on the inside'.

Try this activity with your child. Make it a fun game and see who can make the best faces in front of the mirror:

Practise in front of a mirror 'saying' things with your eyes only.

Try these:

- How very interesting
- I'm bored with this conversation
- How amazing – I'm stunned!
- How long is this going to take?
- I am a cloud
- DON'T EVEN THINK ABOUT IT!

Hold the look until it becomes a stare. It's really good fun. Look into a mirror and try the 'Heavyweight Champion of the World' look, or the Catherine Tate, 'Am I bovver'd?' look. What you need to do is to make sure that you do NOT show your true feelings. The bully wants to have an effect on you. If you give them what they want they will come back time and time again. If you don't, then they will go elsewhere. Remember, we are making sure that *you* are not the victim of the bully.

Have a staring match and see if you can identify what the other is thinking.

Remember that the bully has no right to know what you are feeling inside.

Keep them guessing by hiding your true feelings to them. Practise this until you are really good at it.

Eye gaze game

Maintaining eye contact in our culture and society shows that you have inner strength. It demonstrates self-assurance, and when you look straight into a person's eyes it makes you look more confident.

The child who avoids eye contact may just have not learned this particular social skill, but they will be at a disadvantage until they do.

For those parents who may have exhausted the record, 'Look at me when I talk to you,' here is a fun way to play the eye contact game.

Use a glove puppet and move it to wherever your child is looking, so that it looks as if they are talking to the puppet.

It always gets a laugh and you end up with a smiley child who is also looking into your eyes.

Soon, you will only have to grab the puppet for the exercise to be reinforced.

Maintaining eye contact with the bully is essential.

Other games include staring competitions, pretending that your eyes are laser-destroyers.

5.1.3: Body language collage

This is a very powerful practical exercise which is really good fun and which helps a child to become aware of the power of body language.

It involves making a collage.

You need:

- old children's magazines
- large sheet of paper
- scissors
- glue stick

Working with your child, look through the magazines for examples of children standing or sitting in an assertive way. Point out their eyes and their body posture.

Cut out the ones which appeal to you both and look like pictures of children who are especially confident. Stick them onto the collage and pin it onto the wall in your child's room.

Now encourage your child to stand in front of the picture and imagine that he is all of those children put together.

Ask them: Now how much confidence do you have? How are you standing? Is your head being pulled up to the ceiling by that imaginary string? Absorb their confidence and close your eyes, keeping that confidence inside you.

Now, imagine stepping into the picture and becoming those confident children. See the world from their eyes. Feel what they feel. Open your eyes and enjoy the feeling of confidence and power.

Now write down one aspect of your body language that you can focus on to change:

. . . .

. . . .

Every day for one week, notice how that particular aspect of your body language is behaving.

5.1.4: General body language tips

Do keep your head up. Tilting your head to one side is a show of submission. Face the bully. Don't look down or sideways. Look straight at them and remember to let your eyes say, 'Don't even think about it!'

Make eye contact, stand tall and walk away. Practise this in front of the mirror, say it to the dog, confront the goldfish and surprise your Auntie Flossie, but make sure that you practise it.

If you want to say 'No', say 'No', calmly and firmly. Don't make excuses or try to offer the other person an alternative. Use a strong tone of voice and maintain firm eye contact.

Beware of taking up too little space. Use up as much space as you can. Stand tall and square, not hunched up.

Master the use of the blank, neutral look.

Get your body language right. Always make eye contact, stand tall, smile and walk away.

5.1.5: Our favourite body language tips

....

....

....

....

....

....

....

....

....

....

....

....

....

....

....

5.2: Anti-bullying tricks

5.2.1: 'Bully Bullets'

The trick to the 'bully-bullet' is to redress the balance in a potentially bullying situation. Given a little practice, it will become a very effective part of your child's arsenal against a bully who teases.

Check through the following table and in the spaces, write down the phrases which a bully might have used against your child, e.g., 'you're so fat', or 'four-eyes' etc.

Look at the bully-bullets and agree which ones would work for your child. Change the responses if you wish, using language which is natural to your child and your culture. Practise time and time again, within the security of the family, before unleashing the new skill onto the bully.

Turn it into a game, learning how to use 'banter' to take the sting out of a possibly confrontational situation.

When practising the replies, always use clear, calm, slow and confident speech; make eye contact, stand tall and *always* walk away.

Once your child can use a quick retort in a game, get them to try it out on the bully. Watch the bully become very confused – they won't expect to be answered back.

Fill in the spaces:

Bully's taunt: You're fat.

Bully bullet: Well, thank you for that. You're so kind. I'm clever too.

Bully's taunt: We don't want you to play with us.

Bully bullet: Well, thanks for letting me know; I can play with ………. instead then.

Bully's taunt: I don't like you.

Bully bullet: Well, it's a waste of my time playing with you then
....

Bully's taunt: We don't want you in our group.

Bully bullet: Oh good. I can go and make some new friends then.

Bully's taunt: ....

Bully bullet: You used that tease last week. Can't you think of a new one?

Bully's taunt: ....

Bully bullet: I think you've read the wrong book on how to make friends

Bully's taunt: ....

Bully bullet: Thank you for teaching me how to deal with a bully

Bully's taunt: ....

Bully bullet: Thank you for this training in how to look after myself

Bully's taunt: ....

Bully bullet: If you stop being irritating, I might not report you this time

Bully's taunt: ....

Bully bullet: Try that again and I'll report you to...

Bully's taunt: ....

Bully bullet: True, but I am a genius

Bully's taunt: ....

Bully bullet: I hope you won't keep boring me with this remark every time I see you

Bully's taunt: You're . . . .

Bully bullet: Yes, I know, it's a real gift

Bully's taunt: . . . .

Bully bullet: I've got better things to do than to try to make friends with a bully.

Now have fun making up some of your own. You get the idea – be assertive, without being rude; baffle the bully with your intelligent Bully-bullets and generally turn the encounter into a positive one, *in which the bully is doing you a favour.*

Practise with someone at home until the replies become second nature. Then it's time to unleash your newfound Bully-bullet skills on the bully. Won't they be surprised? They won't know what to do. They will be expecting you to react by being upset, which is exactly what they want.

Remember that a bully is usually a coward, and will not want to stick around if they are not getting the response they want – they'll move off and try to find someone else.

Watch it happening and make sure that you write your successes down in your Success Diary – exactly what they said and how you replied. The trick will come to you even easier the next time - and so on.

Make sure that your Bully-bullet is POSITIVE and lets the bully know that what they are saying is going to lead to a GOOD thing happening for you.

Choose one Bully-bullet at a time to practise – don't try them all at once, or the task will be too much for you and you'll give up.

Practise the Bully-bullets, talking to an empty chair, or your teddy bear. (It works.) You may feel a bit silly, but does it matter? You won't be feeling silly once you are in a Bully-Free Zone.

69

If you use a mixture of replies, the bully will be utterly confused. They will not be getting their predicted response and will leave you alone. All this takes a little practice to become part of your normal language, but it is fun practising it with friends and family. Don't try to learn all of them. Just choose two or three that you feel comfortable with. Once you start getting a result you will want to try more.

Bullies beware.

So here we go with some more Bully-bullet ideas:

- Surprise the bully by agreeing with them. This takes away their power: 'Well thank you for your comments – they really help'; 'Thank you for telling me that – how sweet of you to notice.'
- Shock them by behaving very differently: pretend to vomit in front of them, sing the National Anthem or laugh really loudly at them.
- Use the 'broken record' technique. Say 'no'. But not just once – keep saying it.
- Draw attention to them by shouting within earshot of an adult: 'I don't think you should be bullying me.' They are less likely to bully you again if you embarrass them.
- Interrupt them and start talking about something completely different – make sure that it is something positive. Use disconnected comments such as, 'This is such a fun game, isn't it?'
- Challenge them by asking questions: 'Exactly who said that you could try to bully me like this?' Keep asking the questions and engaging them in conversation.
- Clarify what they are saying to you: 'So what is it that you don't like about me again?'
- Ask them directly what they are trying to do: 'Are you trying to hurt my feelings or are you trying to be my

friend?'

- Match their anger with your sympathy: 'I understand why you are so upset and I would do exactly the same if I were you, but...'
- Baffle them with a confusing reply: 'I know - but why is it green?'
- Use short responses, if you can't think of an immediate reply: 'Great. OK then. So - what? Well I never! Whatever! You're so right'.
- Use the visualisation tricks: pretend to yourself that the bully's taunt is something physical, like a ball kicked at you, which you can dodge, or a laser beam which is deflected because of your force-field.
- Another very good visualization trick is to imagine that you have a mirror force field, which deflects the bully's attack straight back at them.

5.2.2: How to protect yourself when a bully taunts you:

- Look at the bully, straight into their eyes
- Don't get upset or let the bully know how you feel
- Stand still – don't wriggle about
- Maintain a blank, neutral look on your face
- Check your stance – are you standing straight up, with your shoulders straight and square - imagine that a string is attached to the top of your skull and is pulling you up to the sky
- Speak clearly, loudly, slowly and calmly
- Use one of the Bully-bullets that you have practised
- Go straight to a person in authority (parent or teacher) and tell them exactly what has just happened
- Write the incident down in your diary during the evening, including the names of any witnesses

- Ask Mum when you can start karate lessons. If you can actually physically defend yourself, a bully will be able to tell in your body language – and will avoid you.

5.2.3: In the playground

- Don't show the bully you are upset, but do tell them that their behaviour is unacceptable. It's none of their business how you feel. Show your true feelings to your family instead. Bullies love a reaction – don't give them one. If you show the bully that you are upset, then you are rewarding their aggression and it may be exactly what they want to hear to give them a feeling of power.
- If someone physically hurts you, then tell them that you are about to report them and go and do just that.
- Bullying usually occurs where there is very little adult supervision, so make sure that you identify these areas (e.g., toilets or locker areas) and avoid them. Stay where you know there is supervision.
- Don't hit back or abuse them back, even if you have been encouraged to do so by friends or well-meaning family. You will find that you are in as much trouble as they are, if you do.
- If your intuition, your gut instinct tells you that you are in danger, then don't hang around, but get away as soon as possible. Try to baffle the bully, and distract them in order to escape, before going straight to find an adult to help you.
- Don't take expensive items to school. Envy is a major trigger for a bully.

5.2.4: In the classroom

- If a bully is throwing things at you in class, keep all of the

72

objects until you can show the collection to the teacher.

- If someone is stealing things from you or moving your stuff, then report it to a teacher and ask if they can keep a watch out to catch the bully red-handed.
- Telling a teacher: If your teacher has dismissed your problem in the past because they have been too busy, say this: 'I need to talk to you in private. When could you give me ten minutes of your time?' Make sure that you take with you anything which you have written down about the problem. Ask their advice. Say that you really want to do well at school, but that the problem with the bully is preventing you from concentrating and learning. If the teacher still does not listen, get your parents to write to the headteacher, the Chair of Governors and the Local Education Authority.

5.2.5: At home

- Take up karate, tae kwon do or judo. It does wonders for your self-esteem and it means that you can repel an attack without being aggressive.
- Keep a diary or a journal and record events and feelings.
- Write down how you have coped in bullying situations.
- Plan how you will cope in future.
- Do the exercises in Chapter Six of this book!
- Give yourself some happy time and find ways to feel good about yourself.
- Get used to saying affirmations as a way of improving your self-worth and determination to succeed.

5.3: Controlling feelings and emotions

- If you don't feel confident inside, then 'fake it'. After a while it will become part of your behaviour and you won't need to pretend any more. If you appear confident, then people are going to notice and appreciate you – and you will inspire trust and confidence in others.
- Remember that it is the bully who has the problem – not you. You don't need to let them drag you down to their low level.
- Keep away from low-energy people – that means make sure that you surround yourself with the kind of people who have high self-esteem. If you find yourself spending time with a negative person or a moaner, then deliberately move away and find someone who is happy and who will raise your spirits.
- Don't criticise yourself. It reduces your energy and will only drag you down. If you make a mistake, say to yourself that mistakes are the necessary stepping-stones to success. We all have to make mistakes and there's nothing wrong with that. The trick is to make sure that you don't keep making the same mistake over and over again. The biggest mistake you can make in life is to be continually worrying about making one. There is a wonderful quotation from James Joyce, who said, *'mistakes are the portals of discovery.'*
- When negative thoughts creep in, say 'hello' to the thought as if it is a visitor, then 'goodbye', then 'out!' to yourself and feel your brain kicking them out of your head. Say your favourite affirmation and know that you are strong. This might take a bit of practice, but it is so effective if you persevere with it and the technique will remain with you all of your life. **People who are positive thinkers attract friends – those who are negative send them away.**
- If you are bullied, it is not your fault. You don't deserve to

be bullied – ever. Accept, however, that you can be largely responsible for keeping the bully away from you.

- Every moment that you spend being upset or angry because of someone else's behaviour, that is a moment in which you have given up control of your life to the other person. The bully is controlling your life. They are the one with the problem – it is not yours. You do not need the friendship of this person – they are draining you and controlling your life. You will become a non-victim as soon as you stop expecting to be victimised.

5.3.1: How to cope with an angry person: a life skill

Older children will learn an essential life-skill if they can practise this technique:

- Be calm and listen carefully.
- Say to yourself that their anger belongs to them – it isn't yours and they are probably having a go at you because *they have* a problem and you got in the way. You don't have to take it personally.
- Listen to what they are saying and watch what they are doing.
- Look for an opportunity to speak and use their name politely.
- Use your hand in a 'stop' sign.
- At first, speak as loudly as they are doing, but then straight away lower your voice until it is really low and calm. If you practise this, it will become a tool which you can use for the rest of your life.
- Say, 'I understand that you are angry.'
- Repeat back to them what they have just said: 'So you are saying that …' This takes the sting out of their anger and shows that actually you do understand them. Bullies don't

75

expect to be 'understood'.

- Respect yourself by saying that you disagree, if this is so, but say it calmly, after you have told them that you understand why they are angry.
- Stand straight and square; stay tall and confident. Say, 'see you later' and just walk away. Don't get involved and don't let their anger rub off on you. Respect yourself.
- Dealing with angry people is a life-skill. Everybody gets angry sometimes and you will gain a lot of respect if you can stay calm.

5.3.2: How to manage your own anger

This too, is directed to an older child. Of course, sometimes, **you** will feel angry too.

Sometimes being bullied results in some very negative feelings, including anger. Here is a very good way to calm down:

- Breathe in slowly, counting to ten.
- Hold this breath for a count of five.
- Think of a situation in which you were really happy. Imagine you're on holiday, in the pool, floating on a lilo, looking up at the sky.
- Try to hold that feeling.
- Exhale slowly for a count of ten. (You can do it.)
- Count to five before you breathe in again.
- Repeat this cycle a few times.
- You should now feel more calm and in control.

Now think carefully about your choice as to what to do next. You can either get involved or walk away. What is the best thing to do right now? Is getting angry going to improve the situation? No? Good choice.

Whenever you allow yourself to feel anger, you feel weaker for the effort.

Save your energy. Walk away and look for something positive to channel your energies into. Conflict cannot survive without your participation.

5.3.3: How to release negative feelings

- Find somewhere quiet to sit. Breathe deeply.
- Go for a walk in a natural environment, like a park.
- Smile or say hello to someone in the street. Smiling has the power to change your mood [39].
- Do some physical exercise – something which you really like. It could be running, skipping, hitting a punch-bag or kicking a football – whatever you want. Vigorous exercise reduces depression, anxiety and overwhelming negative thoughts [40].
- Sleep on it. Snuggle down with a favourite blanket or soft toy. Sleep resets your capacity to cope with negative emotions [41].
- Play music loudly. Dance to the music – this is a wonderful way to release feelings and end up feeling really good about yourself. Use headphones if your music would disturb someone else.
- Keeping a diary, and writing about how you feel, actually makes you feel better [42]. Always end your diary entry with writing down one really good thing which happened to you today, naming one person who helped you or made you happy. This will help you to see the positive side of life and to look forward to writing in your diary again.
- Avoid combative or addictive electronic games.
- When you feel a negative emotion coming on, say 'STOP' in your head. Imagine that you are booting that feeling out,

like a football, or pouring cold water all over it. Then focus on something positive, and push through the negativity.

- Talk it through with a trusted friend [43]. You feel better if you get your problems off your chest. Say, 'a problem shared is a problem halved'.

5.3.4: Feelings I would like to control

....

....

....

....

....

....

....

....

....

....

....

....

....

....

....

....

....

....

....

5.4: Girls' cliques

One of the most distressing forms of bullying, especially for a girl, is where another girl or group of girls decide to ostracise her and exclude her from the group.

All humans need to belong to a group to one extent or another, but young girls seem to need the support of their friends more than any other group. In our modern society the need to 'belong to the tribe' is as strong as ever. The child who is insecure or lacking in self-esteem needs the support of peers even more and is thus extremely vulnerable to the effects of exclusion.

If your child is being excluded by members of her group, she should:

- Make sure that an adult knows exactly what is happening. Ask a teacher to watch out for the excluding behaviour.
- Try approaching each member of the group individually and pointing out to them what is happening. This type of mean-ness has probably happened to everyone in the group, so they will all know what it feels like.
- Realise that this will give her opportunities to find new friends. Even though she may not feel like it at the moment, this situation really does give her a chance to find new friends. Think about it – are her existing 'friends' being kind to her? Are they really 'friends'? Is there someone else who might be more loyal and more of a true friend?
- Ask her drama teacher to devise a role-play about excluding behaviour and its impact.
- Make sure that she has more than one group of friends and avoid having just one 'best friend'.
- Not share sensitive personal information which a 'friend' could use to turn against her.
- Join a club outside school, to increase her social circle.

- Do some 'spring-cleaning'. Ditch the friendship group which takes it in turns to exclude one member at a time. They are revealing their own insecurities. Find a more stable group of friends.

- Choose some 'fun' friends. Surrounding herself with moody miseries will only drag her down. Better to seek out the ones who are laughing and enjoying themselves.

- Try not to run her life according to what other people think of her. 'Marching to your own drummer' means being an individual – she will gain more respect in the long run. We don't need other people's approval.

- Avoid gossiping herself. It's really tempting to join in, but only those people with a low self-worth need to 'rubbish' others to make themselves feel good. It also damages self-esteem, and causes guilt inside. When someone frequently judges others, they are just demonstrating that they are a person who needs to judge. **You can be sure that the person who is leading the gossip is the most insecure one in the group.**

Sometimes, the taunts and gossip contain a grain of truth, which will make your daughter feel uncomfortable. None of us are perfect and this 'grain of truth' tactic is meant to make her feel powerless. The message is: 'Don't fall for it'. Perfect people must be very boring.

If someone is unpleasant enough to cut her out of their play, does she really want them as a friend? Will she always be able to trust them? If she can't find someone to play with, she can look at it as an opportunity to go and spend some time with herself.

5.5: Cyberbullying

Depending upon your perspective, cyberbullying is becoming a scourge of our time. Unfortunately, the definition and the extent of cyberbullying is changing by the moment, but it is generally accepted to be bullying through electronic means. Our children are becoming more and more vulnerable since it is difficult for them to avoid the electronic world, be it the mobile phone, the tablet, the internet game, chatrooms, photo-sharing, messaging services or social networking sites.

Cyberbullying is very common now and young people are very likely to come across it. It can happen anywhere and at any time, and since we can't police our children's lives 24 hours a day, we need to be aware of the potential dangers and the ways that it can be controlled. In the first edition of this book, it was reported that 25% of children had experienced cyberbullying. Ten years later, that figure has more than doubled [44]. According to NSPCC.org.uk: *'in our latest research with children, four out of five told us they feel social media sites are failing to protect them from pornographic content, self-harm, bullying and hatred'.*

Cyberbullying can take the form of: **harassment** (being offensive, rude, insulting and/or abusive); **denigration** (spreading rumours, sharing real or altered photos in order to humiliate, spreading lies); **flaming** (being abusive in order to incite an argument and cause distress); **impersonation** (using someone's identity or setting up fame identities in order to defame them); **tricking someone** into sharing sensitive images; **stalking** by sending intimidating messages and **social exclusion** (deliberately leaving someone out of a conversation or group).

The Crown Prosecution Service has a useful set of guidelines on prosecuting cyberbullying cases [45], since it is very important to note that most of the above is illegal and there are a number of laws which come into play:

- Protection from Harassment Act 1997
- Criminal Justice and Public Order Act 1994
- Malicious Communications Act 1988
- Communications Act 2003
- Breach of the Peace (Scotland)
- Defamation Act 2013

The sort of bullying crimes which should be reported to the police include harassment, intimidation, threats, abusive phone calls or texts and hate crimes. Each police authority will have a different person to contact, so it's best to put 'how to report bullying in [your town/county/authority]' into an internet search.

5.5.1: Cyberbullying checklist

Your child may be suffering from cyberbullying if:

- They appear unusually anxious after using a phone or gaming device.
- They suddenly avoid using their electronic communication device.
- They appear anxious when their phone rings or a message is signaled.
- They avoid talking about what they are up to online.
- They spend more time with parents than is usual, in comparison with time with their friends.
- They take their computer or phone into their room, in order to respond to messages.
- They hide their phone, or switch it off uncharacteristically.
- They receive messages in the middle of the night which leave them unable to sleep.

5.5.2: Questions to ask your child about cyberbullying

Opening up a discussion about the use of electronic communication and the potential for cyberbullying will enable parents to establish whether or not their children are in danger of being cyberbullied.

Here are some sample questions to get the conversation started:

- Which websites do you and your friends like best?
- Can you be contacted by people you don't know on those sites?
- Have you ever been contacted by someone in this way?
- Have you ever received messages that have upset you?
- What would you do if someone upset you online?
- Are you worried about posts that others have made about you?
- Have you ever had to delete posts?
- What does your school tell you about cyberbullying?
- Do they have rules?
- Do people follow those rules?
- Who would you tell in school if you knew about cyberbullying going on?
- Did you know that we can help you to stop cyberbullying if it is happening to you?

5.5.3: Tips for teens: sexting

Sexting is the practice of sharing intimate photographs with friends or partners.

A few things to think about before you send a photo:

- Would you be happy for the whole world (including your parents, grandma, teachers or the police) to see that photo?

If not, don't send it. Someone wanting to bully you may make that photo go viral – and you can never get it back.

- Ignore requests from anyone else, for explicit or inappropriate pictures of you. They may not always be your friend.
- Respect yourself. You are more than just your body. Giving in to a request for intimate photos will not make you feel better – and they could make you feel anxious, panicky and very stressed.

If you are sent pictures that make you uncomfortable:

- Delete them. Even having them on your phone may get you into trouble.
- Don't share them with others. If you do, you could land up in much trouble.
- Block anyone who makes you feel uncomfortable. Trust your instincts – they are very often right.
- If you are embarrassed to share sexting problems with family or police, there are a number of organisations there to help you anonymously. They include: ChildLine (childline.org.uk); Cybersmile (cybersmile.org); Bullying UK (Tel: 0808 800 2222)

5.5.4: Tips for teens: mobile phone safety

If you are bullied by phone, you should:

- Tell parents straight away.
- Never ignore mobile phone threats, but treat this as a very serious matter.
- Not respond. The bully is trying to control you and by responding, you are giving them exactly what they want. It will make them do it all the more.

- Keep the message as evidence.
- Block the caller.
- Keep a detailed diary of the date, time, caller-ID or the 'unavailable' message.
- Print off the messages if possible.
- If the bullying is anonymous, think through the list of people who might be doing it as you very probably know the person who is sending these calls or messages. They are probably jealous of you and they certainly feel insecure.

In general, to protect yourself, you should:

- Keep your phone locked with a PIN.
- Ensure that you only give your number to family and trusted friends.
- Don't pick up the phone, or answer messages if you can't see the Caller ID.
- Don't send texts or pictures that you would not be comfortable your parents seeing.

5.5.5: Tips for teens: social networking

- Be very careful: It may take you just a minute to type a social networking message, but that message can be out there in cyberspace for ever, whether you delete it or not. This means that your messages may be seen by parents, teachers, university admission boards and prospective employers. Even if you delete your whole account, your words can very often be retrieved, even years later.
- Be careful of sharing your identity: don't post your email address, date of birth, phone number or address.
- Don't post pictures or tag other people unless you have their permission. If they ask you to un-tag them or to

remove their photo, then do so immediately.

- Check your privacy settings. Make them as private as possible. Note that whenever you get a software update, those settings may automatically reset themselves, opening you up to a lack of privacy.
- Change your password regularly and never give it away to anyone – even a friend.
- Check your location settings. Make sure that your parents know how they are set. Do you want everyone to know where you are – including burglars?
- Be careful about saying derogatory things about other people. You never know who will eventually see those posts.
- Be careful about posting and sharing too often. It makes you look needy.
- Don't post when you're upset. Again, it makes you look needy.
- If you are bullied via social networking, report it to the network provider.
- Log out of your account when you leave your computer.
- The Cyberbullying Research Center in the US has some useful *alternative* advice about how to use social networking to your advantage [46]. It's worth looking up on the internet.

5.5.6: Activity for teens

A useful (holiday?) activity for a teenager is to create a resource for other teenagers on the subject of 'How to Stay Safe Online'. This could be a poster for a school corridor, a fact sheet or a quiz. In so doing, the teenager gets to research the problem thoroughly, and as a result will be much better informed themselves. If there is a younger member of the family, they can use this resource to educate them about the dangers of cyberbullying.

5.5.7: Tips for teens: gaming cyber-bullies

- Avoid provocative names. Having a screen-name, 'gamertag', or nickname which stands out as being provocative will show up on the bully's radar, keep a low profile, at least until you are proficient at the game.
- Don't give out personal information. This is a very serious point. Anyone with malicious intent can use real names, phone numbers, home or e-mail addresses, to harass you *or worse.*
- Don't react. Bullies do it for the reaction. They need power and if they don't get a reaction from you – they'll go look for it elsewhere.
- Play the games which have changeable options. Games which enable you to use changeable rules or options help to prevent certain bully tactics, such as eliminating teammates.
- Newbies should start by creating a private game. Make sure that you are playing only with friends you actually know. Arrange the game privately, playing your own exclusive games that permit only your friends to play.
- Choose the sites which have strict rules. Look at the terms and conditions of the game before you play. If they have 'live' moderators and administrators, then it is more likely that the game will be appropriately policed.
- If you are bullied, move on to a different game for a while. Take a break every now and again and try something else. The bully will move elsewhere and you will have learned a valuable lesson about how to deal with bullies.
- Report the bullies. The game administrators want you to stay in the game. It is in their interest to have a safe playing environment.
- Report bugs. Often it is the glitches which enable the bullies to exploit the game system. Reporting these glitches

will also help the administrators to make the environment safer.

- Don't bully back. Your reputation is important on the Internet. Make sure you don't use bully tactics yourself, as this will make the problem worse and have you labelled as a bully too.

5.5.8: Tips for parents of children who may be cyberbullied

- Your child needs to be comforted, rather than judged if they get caught up in a cyberbullying incident. If they can trust you not to judge them, then they are likely to confide in you again.
- Talk to your child calmly – without over-reacting. They need you to be stable and calm, as they are probably feeling very insecure and scared.
- Collect all the evidence together (screenshots, printouts etc.) Depending on the severity of the situation, you will need to share that with the school, the police and/or the internet provider. Keep a diary of events, locations, witnesses etc.
- Report the incident to the internet provider.
- Contact the police if your child is under any actual threat.
- Don't contact the bully or their parents yourself. Leave that up to the school or police.
- Educate your child about the responsibility of the internet provider and how they can report cyberbullying themselves. Find out how to do it specifically on the sites that they frequent.

5.6: Managing school officials

Having sat down with your child and found out exactly what has been happening, your immediate reaction is likely to want to go straight into school. Try to stay calm. Your child needs you to be stable and supportive, to understand how they feel and to come up with a structured plan of action. Reassure your child that the problem can be sorted, without them being victimised any further.

Remember, too, that if you haven't previously spotted it, then possibly the teacher may not have either.

Approaching the school need not be a stressful experience if you:

- bear in mind that you are all on the same side
- approach them in a friendly and non-confrontational manner
- ask if the teacher has noticed that your child is isolated or unhappy
- ask the teacher how you can work *together* to sort things out
- ask if there are any special arrangements in the school such as 'buddy seats', 'listeners' or learning mentors, who might have a specific role in supporting children who become victim to bullies
- encourage the school to try to identify the bullies, so that they can be caught red-handed, rather than have your child be accused of telling tales.

If you have a meeting with the headteacher or teacher, it is important to write a letter of confirmation, to show that you expect to be taken seriously. An example letter is available for you to use in the Appendix section at the end of the book.

In order to ensure that the school takes your case seriously, it is also a good idea to keep a diary of events. A typical layout is also provided for you in the Appendix.

If your child is being bullied, it is your duty to bring it to the attention of the school. Having been a headteacher for many years, I can also say that the need to work together on this issue is paramount. It is very important that you establish from the beginning that you are all on the same side. If your child is being bullied, then you are naturally and understandably upset. You have a right to complain and to expect that the school will act to stop the bullying and ensure that it does not happen again.

Schools are committed to resolving this problem. It is expected that they have an anti-bullying policy, as part of their safeguarding or child protection policy - one which is transparent and available for scrutiny. It will have been sanctioned by the school governors and will be a very important document in the school.

The school's literature (usually to be found on the school website) should detail:

- Who is in charge of the school's anti-bullying policy
- What children should do if they are bullied
- What to expect if they bully someone else in the school
- Where to get help if they are bullied
- How to follow up with a complaint if the issue is not dealt with satisfactorily.

However, in order to set up a collaborative relationship then you need to try to tackle the subject in a constructive and non-aggressive way, even though you are probably very emotional by this stage. It may be that the teachers simply do not know what has been going on. There may be two sides to the story, of which you have not previously been aware. Try not to blame, demand or threaten.

5.6.1: Tips for dealing with schools

- Make an appointment, rather than rush into school. The teacher or headteacher may be busy on other matters and you need to have plenty of time to resolve the issue.
- It might be a good idea to script what you intend to say and take some notes in with you. Often the fewer words you use, the more impact you make.
- Take the diary and any other evidence you have with you.
- Take a notebook to document what is said and what action is being promised.
- Be persistent.
- Ask to see the school's anti-bullying policy, code of conduct, duty of care policy and accident book.
- Collaborate as much as possible and only go down the route of complaint if there is no other line of action left.
- Don't take the situation into your own hands by tackling the bully or their parents.
- Send your record of the meeting to the headteacher (see the example at the back of the book).
- Arrange a follow-up meeting to discuss the action taken and the outcomes.
- Continue to monitor the situation and keep the diary going.
- Continue to support your child in building up their self-esteem.
- If the bullying does not stop, inform the headteacher that you are taking matters further.
- In that case, send a copy of your letters to the Chair of Governors. You can get that address from the school secretary. Don't agree to send the letter to the school. Insist on obtaining the private address. Ask for the bullying problem to be put on the agenda at the next Governors'

meeting.
- Contact your local education authority or academy directorate and find out who is the designated education officer for the school. Send copies of your letters to them.

Some schools have a policy regarding their responsibility for your child's safety on the way to school. Others argue against it. However, if your child is educated at a school, then they have an obligation to attend – so it is not a choice. If they are bullied on the way to school, then the school has a 'duty of care' to keep them safe. If your child is compulsorily wearing a school uniform to and from school, then the school should accept responsibility for this duty of care. Ask to see the school's policy on its 'duty of care' for children travelling to and from the school.

If all else fails and you decide to move to another school, then make sure that you look for a caring school with an effective anti-bullying policy. Ask to see evidence of how they have effectively dealt with bullying in the past. Speak to existing parents and tap into the local grapevine by speaking to the mums and dads who are standing in the playground at the end of the school day.

Finally, if your child is still victimised at the new school, then it is a very good indicator that further action is needed to build up their self-esteem and their assertiveness skills.

If you ultimately choose to educate your child at home, there are support groups and specialist consultants to help you (e.g., www.education-otherwise.org). It may be that all you need is to put some space between the child and the school, and build up their sense of self-worth through success and achievement, before re-joining the mainstream education process at a later stage.

Having taken immediate steps to try to get the school involved, it is important for you to continue to build up your child's resistance, (self-esteem; body language; anti-bullying strategies) so that the bully leaves them alone in future.

5.7: Notes on Chapter Five

. . . .

. . . .

. . . .

. . . .

. . . .

. . . .

. . . .

. . . .

. . . .

. . . .

. . . .

. . . .

. . . .

. . . .

. . . .

. . . .

. . . .

. . . .

. . . .

. . . .

6: Workbook Exercises

The following section provides a workspace for you and your child to practice the exercises referenced in the book.

It's important to make this a special activity, so if you don't want to write in this book, you could go to a discount book shop, buy a special-looking hard-backed note book, call it 'My Success Diary' and choose which of the activities suit your child's circumstances best.

It is also important to make sure that your child only writes positive things.

Occasionally read it through again together and you will be amazed at how much progress they are making.

There are specific exercises for parents, parents with their children, younger children on their own and older children on their own.

The exercises are separate and can be used in any order, and you will find that you return to the exercises which have been particularly effective for your child.

Some of the exercises will be more suitable for children of a different age to your child, so if you think that, for any reason, a particular exercise might be inappropriate for the moment, then skip it and come back to it later if you choose.

You may wish to read through the whole book before devising your individual action plan, or just work your way through it, making a note of which exercises work best and which need to be repeated.

Either way, repetition is the key.

6.1: Declaration

This declaration is to motivate your child to engage with the self-confidence exercises. The space at the bottom is for them to draw a picture of themselves or their family, or even to make up a family crest or motto.

'Today

I have decided to pay attention to being confident

every day for a whole month.

I dedicate this workbook to:

. . . .

Because I intend to enjoy doing the exercises

and know that you will be very proud of me.'

Other people who will be proud of me:

. . . .

. . . .

. . . .

. . . .

. . . .

. . . .

6.2: Diary pages

Here are some ideas for your diary pages. There are lots more in section 4.9.

Date: ....

My affirmation today:

....

....

The Bully bullet that I am going to practise today is:

....

....

The best thing that has happened to me today is:

....

....

Something good that was said about me today was:

....

....

My feelings today:

....

....

....

My plans for tomorrow are:

....

....

....

6.3: Finding the good things

Together with your child write down five things that they do every day which makes them feel good.

This could be riding their bike home from school, playing with a pet, reading with Mum just before they go to sleep, making Dad a cup of tea in the morning.

....

....

....

....

....

Now write down four more things that are *possible* within your family routines, things your child does not do at the moment but which they would like to do to make themselves feel good.

Agree that you will help them to do them.

They could be such things as helping to make tea once a week, reading their favourite magazine together or watching a sport with Mum or Dad instead of something that they usually do on their own.

This is what I am going to do to make myself happier:

....

....

....

....

....

6.4: Mindset practice

Use this exercise to work together with your child to change any *fixed* mindsets into *growth* mindsets[32]:

Fixed Mindset: I don't think I can do it because I don't have the talent.

Growth Mindset: Perhaps I can't do it now, but I may be able to, if I put in the time and effort.

Fixed Mindset: If I fail, then I'll be called a failure.

Growth Mindset: Every successful person had lots of failures on the way. If they hadn't failed, they wouldn't have eventually succeeded.

Fixed Mindset: If I don't try, then no one will know that I can't do it.

Growth Mindset: If I don't try then I won't give myself a chance to succeed.

Fixed Mindset:

....

Growth Mindset:

....

Fixed Mindset:

....

Growth Mindset:

....

6.5: Changing self-beliefs

Existing 'faulty' belief: I am different from others and people don't like me

New positive belief: I am glad that I am different and that makes me very lovable

Existing 'faulty' belief: I deserve to be bullied because I am no good at anything

New positive belief: I understand why I have been bullied, but that's going to stop now

Existing 'faulty' belief: Nobody will ever stop the bullying

New positive belief: The ideas in this book have worked for other children, and they can work for me too.

Existing 'faulty' belief:

....

New positive belief:

....

Existing 'faulty' belief:

....

New positive belief:

....

Existing 'faulty' belief:

....

New positive belief:

....

6.6: My Success Bank

These are all the positive things people have said to me or about me this week:

....

....

....

....

....

....

....

....

....

....

....

....

....

....

....

....

....

....

....

6.7: The Golden Light of Confidence

Draw a cartoon picture of yourself with the golden confidence light pouring into you, surrounding you and forming an impenetrable shield.

Choose an affirmation to put into a speech bubble:

6.8: What are your future dreams?

Draw two clouds and inside them, write down your greatest dreams.

6.9: My Future Diary

This is a brilliant exercise for re-programming your child's self-image. Read this together:

Imagine that you are in the future.

All the bullying has stopped and life is really fun.

Write an imaginary entry into your future diary about what happened:

Dear Diary,

Today was great!

....

....

....

....

....

....

....

....

....

....

....

....

....

....

6.10: Don't even think about it

Draw a cartoon picture of yourself, saying, 'Don't even think about it!'

6.11: Worthiness exercise

When speaking to someone who might be trying to gain power over you, remember to tell yourself that you are as worthy as the other person.

If you believe in yourself, it will show in your body language and other people will believe in you too.

Use one of these affirmations, and add some of your own:

'I have great confidence in myself.'

'I am a good person.'

'My bully-proof shield is activated.'

....

....

....

....

....

....

....

....

....

....

....

....

....

....

6.12: If I knew I could not fail

Write down two things you would do, if you knew you could not fail:

1. ....

2. ....

What would you have to **do** to achieve these goals?

....

....

....

....

....

....

....

....

....

....

....

....

....

....

....

Do something *every day* towards making it happen.

6.13: My anti-bullying action plan

In this exercise, you have an opportunity to write down all of the ways in which bullies try to upset you.

Now go back through this book and decide how you are going to deal with each of them.

Choose the best response which will work for you.

This is your action plan.

One month later, look at this list again.

Does the plan need to change?

How the bully upsets me:

....

....

....

....

....

....

What I am going to do about it:

....

....

....

....

....

....

How the bully upsets me:

....
....
....
....
....

What I am going to do about it:

....
....
....
....
....

How the bully upsets me:

....
....
....
....
....

What I am going to do about it:

....
....
....
....
....

6.14: My 'How to be Happy' Action Plan

In this exercise, you have an opportunity to write down your favourite *How to Be Happy* tips. Have a look at section 4.5 and choose your favourites, changing the language if necessary:

....

....

....

....

....

....

....

....

....

....

....

....

....

....

....

....

....

....

....

6.15: My favourite affirmations

In this exercise, you have an opportunity to write down your favourite *Affirmations*. Have a look at section 4.2.1 and choose your favourites, changing the language if necessary:

....

....

....

....

....

....

....

....

....

....

....

....

....

....

....

....

....

....

....

6.16: Oh what are we going to do?

This is an opportunity to step back and see a bullying situation from someone else's perspective.

Imagine that your friend is being bullied.

Using what you have learned in this book, can you give them your best anti-bully tips to stop them from being bullied?

....

....

....

....

....

....

....

....

....

....

....

....

....

....

....

....

6.17: My favourite bully-bullets

In this exercise, you have an opportunity to write down your favourite *Bully Bullets*. Have a look at section 5.2.1 and choose your favourites, changing the language if necessary:

. . . .

. . . .

. . . .

. . . .

. . . .

. . . .

. . . .

. . . .

. . . .

. . . .

. . . .

. . . .

. . . .

. . . .

. . . .

. . . .

. . . .

. . . .

. . . .

. . . .

. . . .

6.18: A message to a bully (of any age):

We all need friends. The message could not be clearer: the way to make friends is to be friendly.

You may feel that you need to exert power over others and that you will gain respect this way. If you understand this message right now, you will save yourself from a lifetime of loneliness: what you are doing by bullying is achieving the exact opposite of what you want. You are demonstrating that you are lacking in character; you are losing the respect of others and you could find it very difficult to get it back. **But this needn't be so.**

If you want power, please realise that you can have the most awesome power by helping other children to feel good about themselves – how much better does *that* feel? Walk down the corridor and say hello to one of your previous victims, using their name, smiling with a genuine concern for their happiness. Ask them about their lives. See how many friends you start to gather this way. Today, you could use your power to change a victim into a friend. What an incredible opportunity you have!

The kind of person who attracts friends is unselfish and giving, and always puts being kind above the need for personal gain.

Learn this really important message now and change from being a bully into a friend-magnet. Good luck.

Note: If you know a bully, photocopy this page and give it to them straight! The world will be a better place with one less bully. In this day and age, bullying should not be happening to your child. They don't deserve it.

Let's do what we can to stop it right now.

7: Appendices

7.1: Diary of events

Name of Child:

....

Date of incident

....

Place:

....

Bully's name:

....

Witnesses:

....

....

Reported to:

....

Resolved / unresolved

Action taken:

....

....

Follow up:

....

....

....

7.2: Letter to the school

[Your address here]

[The date here]

[Name of headteacher]

[School address and postcode]

.

Dear [Name of headteacher]

Re: [Name of child]

Thank you for seeing me yesterday about [name of child].

If you recall, I was concerned about the following incident/s which has/have happened in school:

We agreed to ...

You said you would monitor the situation and ...

Please can we have a meeting in two weeks' time, to discuss the situation further? Please put a copy of this letter onto my child's file and let me have a copy of the school's bullying policy.

Yours sincerely,

7.3: Letter to the Chair of Governors

[Your address]

[Date]

To: Chair of Governors

[Name of school]

[Address of school]

Dear Chair of Governors,

Re: Bullying of [name of child]

Having contacted the school regarding the bullying of my child, I am disappointed that the bullying issues have not yet been resolved and that the bullying is still taking place.

Please would you:

- let me know when I can meet you to discuss this problem
- put bullying on the agenda for the next Governors' Board meeting

I await your urgent response.

Yours faithfully,

8: References

[1] http://bit.ly/2ahtJT1

[2] kidscape.org

[3] www.bullying.co.uk

[4] http://bit.ly/2tVBepm

[5] nobullying.com

[6] For a full list of cyberbullying terms, and their definitions, see: nobullying.com

[7] beyondbullies.org

[8] https://www.stopbullying.gov/ what-is-bullying/index.html

[9] Fekkes, M., Pijpers, F.I.M. and Verloove-Vanhorick, S.P. (2005) Bullying: who does what, when and where? Involvement of children, teachers and parents in bullying behaviour. *Health Education Research*. 20 (1): 81-91.

[10] http://files.eric.ed.gov/fulltext/ED543705.pdf

[11] Vaillancourt, T., Hymel, S & McDougall, P. (2003) Bullying is power. *Journal of Applied School Psychology*. 19 (2).

[12] Cohen, A. R. (1959). Situational structure, self-esteem, and threat-oriented reactions to power. In D. Cartwright (Ed.), *Studies in social power* (pp. 35-52). Oxford, England: Univer. Michigan.

[13] See [9]

[14] See [9]

[15] https://www.ditchthelabel.org/ annual-bullying-survey-2016/#download

[16] O'Moore, M. & Kirkham, C. (2001) Self-esteem and its relationship to bullying behavior. *Aggressive Behavior*. Volume 27(4) Pages 269 – 283.

[17] Patchin, J.W. and Hinduja, S. (2010) *Cyberbullying and self-esteem.* Journal of School Health. 80 (12) 614 – 621.

[18] Gendron, B.P., Williams, K.R. & Guerra N.G. (2011) An Analysis of Bullying Among Students Within Schools: Estimating the Effects of Individual Normative Beliefs, Self-Esteem, and School Climate. *Journal of School Violence.* 10 (2) 150 – 164.

[19] Roland, E. (2002) "Bullying, depressive symptoms and suicidal thoughts." *Educational Research.* 44.1: 55-67.

[20] Seals D, Young J. (2003) Bullying and victimization: prevalence and relationship to gender, grade level, ethnicity, self-esteem, and depression. *Adolescence.* 38 (152): 735 - 47.

[21] See [16]

[22] See [16]

[23] Crick, N.R. and Grotpeter, J.K. (1995) Relational aggression, gender and social-psychological adjustment. *Child Development*, 66, 710 – 722.

[24] Wolke, D., Woods, S., Bloomfield, L. and Karstadt, L. (2000) The association between direct and relational bullying and behaviour problems among primary school children. *Journal of Child Psychology and Psychiatry and Allied Disciplines*, 41, 989–1002.

[25] Guerin, S. & Hennessy, E. (2002) Pupils' definitions of bullying. *European Journal of Psychology of Education.* 17(3), 249-261.

[26] Li, Q. (2007) New bottle but old wine: A research of cyberbullying in schools. *Computers in Human Behavior.* 23(4), 1777 – 1791.

[27] Besag, V. (1989). *Bullies and victims in schools.* Milton Keynes: Open University Press.

[28] Smith, P.K., Sharp, S. (1994) In: Smith, P.K., Sharp, S. eds. *School bullying: insights and perspectives.* London: Routledge

[29] Randall, P. (1997). *Adult Bullying: Perpetrators and Victims*. London: Routledge.

[30] Steele, C. M. (1988). The psychology of self-affirmation: Sustaining the integrity of self. In L. Berkowitz (Ed.), *Advances in experimental social psychology* (Vol. 21, pp. 261–302). New York: Academic.

[31] www.louisehay.com/ the-power-of-affirmations/

[32] Dweck, C. S. (2008) *Mindset: the new psychology of success*. New York: Ballantine Books. MLA.

[33] How not to talk to your kids: Retrieved on 27.7.17 from: http://nymag.com/news/features/27840/index1.html

[34] Sheila White (2004) A psychodynamic perspective of workplace bullying: containment, boundaries and a futile search for recognition, British Journal of Guidance & Counselling, 32:3, 269-280

[35] Fritson, K.K. (2008) Impact of Journaling on Students' Self-Efficacy and Locus of Control. *InSight: A Journal of Scholarly Teaching*. 3: 75 – 83.

[36] https://www.ted.com/talks/ amy_cuddy_your_body_language_shapes_who_you_are

[37] Journal of Personality and Social Psychology, Trends in Cognitive Sciences, Psychological Science, Research in Organizational Behavior, Advances in Experimental Social Psychology, and Science

[38] Garrison, K.E., Tang, D. & Schmeichel, B.J. (2016). Embodying power a preregistered replication and extension of the power pose effect. *Social Psychological and Personality Science*.

[39] https://www.scientificamerican.com/ article/smile-it-could-make-you-happier/

[40] https://www.psychologytoday.com/ blog/the-athletes-way/201602/combining-aerobic-exercise-and-meditation-reduces-depression

[41] Van der Helm, E & Walker, M.P. (2009) Overnight Therapy? The Role of Sleep in Emotional Brain Processing. *Psychol Bull.* 135(5): 731–748.

[42] http://newsroom.ucla.edu/ releases/Putting-Feelings-Into-Words-Produces-8047

[43] Adams, R. E., Santo, J. B., & Bukowski, W. M. (2011). The presence of a best friend buffers the effects of negative experiences. *Developmental Psychology, 47*(6), 1786-1791.

[44] http://www.bullying.co.uk/ cyberbullying/what-is-cyberbullying/

[45] http://www.cps.gov.uk/ consultations/social_media_consultation.pdf

[46] https://cyberbullying.org/ smart-social-networking.pdf

9: Further reading

Adams, A. (1992) *Bullying at Work: How to Confront it and Overcome it.* London: Virago Press.

Arora, C.M.J., & Thompson, D.A. (1987) Defining bullying for a secondary school. *Education and Child Psychology,* 4, 110-120.

Bentley, H. *et al.* (2017) *How safe are our children? The most comprehensive overview of child protection in the UK.* Retrieved on 14.8.17 from: https://www.nspcc.org.uk/services-and-resources/research-and-resources/2017/how-safe-are-our-children-2017/.

Beran, T. & Li, Q. (2004) *Is Cyber-Harassment a Significant Problem? A Report On Children's Experiences.* Calgary: University of Calgary.

Beran, T. & Li, Q. (2005) Cyber-Harassment: A New Method for an Old Behavior, *Journal of Educational Computing Research* 32(3), 265–277.

Bjorkqvist, K. & Osterman, K. (1999) Finland. In: Smith, P.K. et al. (Eds), *The Nature of Bullying: a Cross National Perspective* (pp. 56 67). London: Routledge.

Davies, B. (2003) Frogs and snails and feminist tales. *Preschool children and gender* 2nd ed., Cresskill, NJ: Hampton Press.

Engels, R. (2001) Self-esteem and its relationship to bullying behaviour. *Aggressive Behavior.* 27(4), 269-283.

Field, E.M. (2010) *Bully blocking at work. A self-help guide for employees and managers.* Australian Academic Press.

Galloway, D. and Roland, E. (2004) Is the direct approach to reducing bullying always the best? *In Bullying in schools: How successful can interventions be?* Edited by: Smith, P.K., Pepler, D. and Rigby, K. Cambridge: Cambridge University Press.

Guerin, S., & Hennessy, E. (1998) Student Perceptions and Definitions of Bullying: A Question of Methodology. In D. Hogan

& R. Gilligan (Eds.), *Researching Children's Experiences: Qualitative Approaches.* Children's Research Centre, Trinity College Dublin.

Guerin, S., & Hennessy, E. (2001) Examining reported involvement in bullying in Irish primary schools. *Journal of Child-Centred Practice,* 8(1), 55-68.

Guerin, S., & Hennessy, E. (2000) Aggression and Bullying. *BPS Parent, Adolescent and Child Training Skills Series.* London; Blackwell.

Josephs, R., Markus, H., & Tafarodi, R. (1992) Gender and self-esteem. *Journal of Personality and Social Psychology,* 63, 391-402.

Kaltiala-Heino, R., Rimpelae, M., Marttunen, M., Rimpela, A. & Rantanen, P. (1999) Bullying and suicidal ideation in Finnish adolescents: school survey. *British Medical Journal,* 319, 348-351.

M. O'Moore and C. Kirkham (2001) Self-esteem and its relationship to bullying behavior. *Aggressive Behavior.* 27(4), 269–283.

Namie, G. & Namie, R. (2000) *The Bully at Work: What You Can Do to Stop the Hurt and Reclaim Your Dignity on the Job.* Naperville: Sourcebooks.

Olweus, D. (1993) *Bullying: What we know and what we can do.* Oxford: Blackwell Publishers.

Olweus, D. (1994) Bullying at School: Basic facts and effects of a school-based intervention programme. *Journal of Child Psychology and Child Psychiatry,* 35(7), 171-1190.

Olweus, D. (1997) Bully/victim problems in school. *Irish Journal of Psychology,* 18(2), 170-190.

Randall, P. (1997) *Adult Bullying: Perpetrators and Victims.* London: Routledge.

Rayner, C. (1999) From research to implementation: finding leverage from prevention. *International Journal of Manpower,* 20(1,2), 28-38.

122

Rigby, K. (1997) *Bullying in schools and what to do about it,* Melbourne: Australian Council for Educational Research.

Roland, E. (2002) Bullying, depressive symptoms and suicidal thoughts. *Educational Research.* 44(1), 55-67.

Seals D. & Young J. (2003) Bullying and victimization: prevalence and relationship to gender, grade level, ethnicity, self-esteem, and depression. *Adolescence.* 38(152),735-47.

Swain, J. (1998). What does bullying really mean? *Educational Research,* 40(3), 358-364.

Smith, P.K., & Levan, S. (1995). Perceptions and experiences of bullying in younger pupils. *British Journal of Educational Psychology,* 65, 489-500.

Smith, P.K., & Sharp, S. (1994). The problem of school bullying. In P.K. Smith & S. Sharp (Eds.), *School bullying: Insights and perspectives* (pp. 2-19). London: Routledge.

Stephenson, P., & Smith, D. (1989). Bullying in the junior school. In D.P. Tattum & D.A. Lane (Eds.), *Bullying in school* (pp. 45-57). Stoke-on-Trent: Trentham Books.

Wenxin, Z. (2002) Definitions of bullying: a comparison of terms used, and age and gender differences, in a fourteen-country international comparison. *Child development.* 73(4), 1119-33.

White, S. (2004) A psychodynamic perspective of workplace bullying: containment, boundaries and a futile search for recognition, *British Journal of Guidance & Counselling,* 32(3), 269-280.

10: Emergency numbers

If you suspect that a child needs this page, then let them see this:

If an adult bullies you by trying to get you to do something you are not comfortable with, then you need to get help immediately.

Tell someone you trust or ring:

Childline: 0800 1111 in the UK

https://www.childline.org.uk

or 1-800-422-4453 (ChildHelp) in the US

https://www.childhelp.org

In an emergency, ring

999 in the UK

911 in the US

112 in Europe

Intentionally left blank

Printed in Great
Britain
by Amazon